HOW TO START YOUR 'HOME FROM HOME' DOG BUSINESS

The Kickstarter's Survival Guide To Doggy Bliss

(Incorporates The Animal Welfare (England) Regulations 2018)

Randle Stonier, Co-Founder of MyWaggyTails

For Mitch, David and Ebs – who've shared the journey.

Thank you.

Table of Contents

Chapter 1

Introduction

Welcome to **'Home from Home'** – your guide to escaping a job that sucks and starting a new career with canine clients.

If you're a dog lover that is considering opening your home to canine clients for either home boarding and/or home day care, this is the book for you. Within the pages of this tome, you'll find all the information you could possibly hope for to make your business a success – and a little more besides.

I have long considered writing this book, and finally decided to do so for a number of reasons. My primary intention is to help more and more people realise their dreams, and to make a living doing what they love. Namely, working with dogs from home.

Now, as you'll learn throughout this book, this is not an easy life. Working with dogs isn't for the faint-hearted, and there will be a number of challenges along the way. Thankfully, when you're looking into a pair of big brown eyes and watching a tail thump in happiness, all of those difficulties will melt away.

Together with my sister, Mitch I've been through this experience. Several times over, in fact. This means that I know how difficult it can be. If you can learn from our mistakes, you won't make the same missteps. Equally, you can put our techniques that have proved successful into practice, and fast track your business to the top tier.

So, what will you learn from this book? All kinds of things! As a summary of what I'll be covering, the coming pages will discuss...

Is a dog business right for you? Before you go any further, you need to be certain of what you're getting into. Working with dogs is fabulous, but it's not always easy. There will be a range of considerations - legal and personal - that you'll need to take under advisement before committing to this line of work.

What will you earn, and how much will it cost you? Naturally, there is no hard and fast answer to this. How much money you can make depends on how much work you put into building your business, and how many dogs you can take on based on the size of your property. You should be aiming to make between £5-7.5k annually for each dog that you take into your home. And unless you are just doing this for pin money you need to aim to be licensed for five guest dogs as a minimum. As a wise businessperson once said, however, you'll need to speculate to accumulate. You'll need to pay for home improvements, licenses and insurance policies, as well as saving up for the dreaded tax bill every January.

How to get started. There's a whole lot that you'll need to consider before you can open the doors of your business. There are home improvements to be made, inspections to be had, possibly permits to apply for, and a great deal of learning to do. I'll take you through the earliest days of your canine enterprise, ensuring that you can hit the ground running as soon as you're ready.

The legal stuff. One of the toughest parts of running your own business is staying on top of legal and financial regulations. I'm not a lawyer or accountant, and I won't pretend otherwise. However, I do have a working knowledge of what you'll be up against that I'm more than willing to share – and I can certainly signpost you in the right direction for professional help and assistance.

Managing client expectations. If there's one downside to working with dogs, it's the fact that they come with human owners. They need to be appeased too, and that takes more than a biscuit and a scratch behind the ears. I'm being tongue-in-cheek of course, but this is important. You'll need to ensure that you have firmly defined policies in place to make your business a success.

What your day will entail. Collect dog, play with dog, return dog, count money? If only it was that simple. Your doggy business will constantly keep you on your toes, and I'll discuss what you may be able to expect on a typical day. Spoiler warning – no two days will ever be the same.

Building and maintaining your business. If you're going to be a success, you'll need to strike the fine balancing act of constantly attracting new customers, while also keeping your existing client base happy. I'll explain how you can do this and continue building your business empire.

Of course, I'll also discuss dogs throughout. From boisterous puppies to lethargic pension-drawing pooches, every single dog is different. There will be a base knowledge that's absolutely essential for you, though. I'll discuss dog training techniques, the etiquette of walkies, how to manage problem behaviour, and so much more.

Are you eager to get started? I hope so. That's enough from me for now - turn the page and begin your dog business adventure. I'm with you every step of the way.

Randle

Chapter 1

Understanding the Lingo

First thing's first - if you plan to run a canine boarding or day care business, you'll need to know exactly what that entails. The vocabulary that you use is very important, as even a minor, inadvertent discrepancy could unwittingly land you in trouble with the law. Forgiveness is in short supply where bureaucracy is concerned.

Before you read anything else in this book, you should bookmark this page and pull up your computer. You're going to need to research the rules and regulations that surround canine welfare in the UK. This may sound like a simple Google search, but there's more to it than that. At the time of writing, England has different regulations from the other three home nations. This is because the countries are governed by different legislation.

Citizens of Wales and Scotland must abide by the laws established in the Animal Boarding Establishments Act of 1963 and Northern Ireland by the Animal Boarding Establishments Regulations 1974. Even then, there are local authorities who have chosen to adopt the LACORS model framework, and those that haven't – just to complicate matters. Patchwork quilt anyone?

However, in the words of the act itself, "For the purpose of this act the keeping of such establishments is defined as the carrying on at any premises, including a private dwelling, of a business of providing accommodation for other people's cats and dogs."

If you're in England, you'll be subject to the Animal Welfare (Licensing of Activities Involving Animals) (England) Regulations of 2018, which is an offshoot of the Animal Welfare Act of 2006. Again, let's quote Her Majesty (albeit through her governmental proxies) - "The Animal Welfare Act 2006 makes owners and keepers responsible for ensuring that the welfare needs of their animals are met."

This sounds pretty standard. If you're not planning on meeting the welfare needs of the dogs in your care, you're really looking at the wrong business. In addition, most of the additions to the Animal Welfare (Licensing of Activities Involving Animals) (England) Regulations centre around breeders, and the welfare and sale of young dogs. Essentially, they are in place to put a stop to puppy farming. That's something that we can all get behind.

We can possibly expect that the remaining home nations will move towards adopting England's most recent regulations in the near future. Depending on when you read this book, they may have already done so. Or maybe they won't. The important thing to know is that there is plenty of crossover between the laws, so the subjects that I'll discuss throughout these pages are relevant to everybody.

The key rules of the Animal Boarding Establishments Act of 1963 and Animal Welfare (Licensing of Activities Involving Animals) (England) Regulations 2018 are as follows:

- Nobody can run a canine boarding business without the appropriate certification and licensing, bestowed at the discretion of a local authority. This license can be refused if the requester is disqualified from owning or working with animals.
- Your home must meet the needs of your canine clients. To quote the legislation, this means that:
  - The animals will at all times be kept in accommodation suitable as respects construction, size of quarters, number of occupants, exercising facilities, temperature, lighting, ventilation and cleanliness.
  - The animals will be adequately supplied with suitable food, drink and bedding material, adequately exercised, and (so far as necessary) visited at suitable intervals.
  - All reasonable precautions will be taken to prevent and control the spread among animals of infectious or contagious diseases, including the provision of adequate isolation facilities.
  - Appropriate steps will be taken for the protection of the animals in case of fire or other emergency.
  - A register must be kept containing a description of any animals received into the establishment, date of arrival and departure, and the name and address of the owner, such register to be available for inspection at all times by an officer of the local authority, veterinary surgeon or veterinary practitioner.
- Your local authority can request an inspection of your business premises at any time to ensure that the dogs are being cared for appropriately. Refusing this inspection, or wilfully obstructing it without good reason, is a criminal offense.
- If you have pets of your own, you must obtain written acknowledgement from your clients that they know this and remain happy for their own dog to board with you. They must also provide consent for their dog(s) to be boarded with, fed

(or not) and walked with dogs from other households, as well as approving exercise off-leash.

- You cannot take in any canine whose breed is listed under the Dangerous Dogs Act of 1991, even if the owner of the dog has an exemption certificate. For the avoidance of doubt, these breeds are:
    - Pit Bull Terrier
    - Japanese Tosa
    - Dogo Argentino
    - Fila Brasileiro
- You cannot take in a puppy that has yet to be vaccinated. Neither should you want to.
- All dogs under your care must be allowed to exercise twice a day, for a minimum of 20 minutes. Yes, that means walkies. The good news is that this could be a potential additional revenue stream. You could take on additional dog walking customers and exercise their pets alongside those in your charge, if they all get along (and you have written consent). I'll discuss the logistics of dog walking in a professional capacity elsewhere in this tome.

So, in summary, you cannot board any dog breed deemed dangerous, you must have the appropriate licenses in place, you need to keep very strict records, you just walk the dogs, and your home must be declared canine safe by the standards of a professional. If you are wondering what 'suitable accommodation' actually means, follow these guidelines:

- Every dog must have access to a designated private room for a time out if needed. This room should have a window that opens but remains secure. The floor area needs to be a minimum of twice the length of the dog, on all directions. The room should also not be occupied by a child under the age of 16.
- The dogs cannot be locked in the garden all day, but they must be able to get outside I f they wish to. This means that you'll also need to ensure that your garden is safe and secure.

Take these regulations seriously. You can be fined up to £2,500 or imprisoned for up to 3 months – or both, if you're particularly unfortunate – if you break any of these laws.

If any person aged under 16 years resides at the home, there must be procedures in place to regulate the interactions between the dogs and that person.

So, you're now completely *au fait* with the law and ready to get started, right? Not quite, I'm sorry to say. We now have to take a detailed look at what 'dog boarding' actually means, according to the letter of the law. Using the 2018 regulations laid out in England, the terminology breaks down in the following way.

- **Home Boarding** involves dogs staying in your home for over 14 hours – usually, as long as a week or two weeks. Essentially, if you're looking to run a home boarding business, it means that you are inviting dogs to become a part of your family for a contractually agreed period of time. The majority of your home boarding clients will be business travellers or families that are taking a holiday, but do not wish to leave their beloved pet in kennels.
- **Home Day Care** is slightly different. This means that you'll be taking care of a dog during daylight hours, but they won't be spending the night. Perhaps the dog will spend the hours of 7am to 6pm with you from Monday to Friday, for example. Expect this service to be very popular if you live in a commuter belt. Basically, it's pet sitting. Except it's not.
- **Pet Sitting**, from a legal standpoint, involves taking care of one or two dogs from the same household, either in your own home of that of the dogs. You'll need a license for pet sitting if you accept any kind of payment for this activity, unless your income totals less than £1,000 PA. If you have no other income other than pet sitting, you are not obliged to disclose your earnings to HMRC.
- **Pet Home Visits** are very short-term stops at the home of the dog. Ordinarily, you'd spend up to an hour in the dog's home if fulfilling this service. The purpose of this definition is somebody that pops in to top up a water bowl, take the dog for a leg-stretch, and generally keep the lonely pooch company for a little while. This falls under the same regulations as pet sitting. Pet home visits are popular for families with old or young pets that do not mix well with others, dogs recovering from operations that need rest but still require company and care and bitches that are currently in heat and will send other dogs into a frenzy. You may also be asked to feed and care for other pets at the same time, such as rabbits or cats. It's at your discretion as to whether you'll engage with a python or tarantula.
- **Commercial Day Care** applies to readers with particularly large properties. If you have a bespoke doggy day care premises on a large area of land or a converted industrial unit, taking in dogs in substantial quantities (I'm talking 25, 50 or even 100 at a time), you'll need a Commercial Day Care license.

Something to bear in mind here is that the definition of your business venture and the rules of the game can be open to interpretation by your local authority. This means that it's best to err on the side of caution, and have a full, frank and open conversation before applying for a licence.

It can be worryingly easy to commit a legal offense, and pleading ignorance – while understandable, and likely accurate – will not get you very far. Don't end up on the hook for a fine. Ensure that everything is above board (no pun intended), and you have covered every possible activity that you will be undertaking as part of your business.

Still with me? Great! I have an important question that I need to put to you, though. The potential success of your business depends on how your answer it, so give it some thought.

Did that sound dramatic? Hope so. Turn the page to see the question.

Chapter 2

Is a Dog Business Right for You?

Before I go any further, it's critical that we establish that a dog business is the right choice for you. Many people enter this realm of work with the best of intentions, but somewhat naïve expectations. That's a fast track to insanity, and something that we're all keen to avoid.

I have news for you. Dog boarding businesses are not an easy way to make money. If you're going to be successful, you need to focus on one key word. No, not dog. This is one time that dogs will not be at the centre of your universe.

I mean *business*. If you're going to make this work, you need to think like a businessperson. That means understanding everything that running a dog boarding service entails – and answering some tough questions along the way.

Why Dogs?

The first question you need to ask yourself is why you wish to open your home to dogs.

If you answered that with, "because dogs are great!" then I'm inclined to agree with you. Dogs make wonderful company. Here's the thing, though - dogs can also be *really* hard work. Never turn your home into a dog boarding business on the assumption that it will be easier than running a B&B, or a day care centre for human children. Our tail wagging chums are just as capable of wearing down your last nerve, and wreaking havoc everywhere they go. If I'm to be completely honest, isn't that what we love *most* about them?

Dogs can bring a welcome slice of mischief into anybody's life, and that's surely something to celebrate. All the same, your canine clients may be a troublesome bunch on occasion. You really need to know what you're getting into. There's more to running a dog business than simply tickling adorable puppy tummies all day.

Now, you may be wondering why I'm taking this tack so early. After all, surely you know that you want to work with dogs. Why else would you have laid down your hard-earned money for this book, and carved out some precious time in your schedule to read it?

I want to make sure that *your* business is a success. This means that I want you to know exactly what you're letting yourself in for, and understanding what will be involved. Working with dogs is fun, rewarding, and entertaining. It's also messy, frustrating, and on occasion, heart-breaking. Basically, it's very similar to working with kids. There's a reason why people say it takes a particular temperament to work with children and animals.

So, with all of this in mind, I'll ask again. Why do you want to work with dogs?

Is it because you want the freedom of running your own business? That's a great explanation. However, there are a number of different business plans that will not require cleaning poop from your carpet (at least not in a literal sense), walking for hours outside in the rain, and explaining to your spouse how their treasured family heirloom was shattered into a thousand pieces. Never make the mistake of assuming that doggy day care is the easiest way to get a solo venture off the ground.

Is it because you want to work from home? Again, a very noble intention. Just remember, when your home becomes your workplace, there is no escaping your business. Your living room is now your office, your bedroom is now your boardroom, and your bathroom ... well, it's probably best to leave that as a bathroom. The kind of business that gets conducted in there is a private activity.

However, the reality is that your home *will* become open season for your canine clients, their human owners, and any relevant authorities. You could be inspected at any time, you will have strangers wandering around your home, and nothing you own will be yours any longer. And that's before some lovely dog decides to 'mark' it as his or her own.

Is it because you think that running your own business will be easier to fit into your schedule? On paper, that's true. In reality, however, you will run into all kinds of potential kinks. The owners of the dogs in your care may be delayed in collecting their pets – flight cancellations, leaves on the rail line or the wrong kind of snow, for example. It's not like you can leave the animals unattended while you run errands and collect the kids from school. You'll need to have contingency plans in place.

Is it because you've read that the UK is a nation of dog lovers, and this is sure fire way to make money? Well, you got that half right. We are certainly crazy about canines here in Blighty. Every dog owner wants their four-legged friend to have the best life possible, and that may involve arranging day care while they work long hours. Pampered pooches become accustomed to a certain lifestyle, and that's not cheap to maintain. All the same, running a dog boarding business isn't as simple as opening your back door and counting £50 notes. To be successful, you're going to need to roll up your sleeves and put the work in.

Is it because you already have a dog, and you like the idea of them having a little company of his or her own kind? That's sweet of you. Has your dog spent prolonged periods of time with other canines before, though? There's a big difference between a five-minute play in the park and spending all day with other dogs. Your dog will need to learn how to share and accept that they cannot be the centre of attention at all times. In addition, you'll also need to make sure that your clients don't mind their dogs sharing their day with a resident pet.

Is it because you can't think of anything else to do with your time, and hey, hanging out with dogs all day sounds fun? Oh, my sweet summer child. Have you learned nothing from our warnings thus far? This line of work *is* fun, but it's also a lot of effort. If you consider work to be the wrong kind of four-letter word, this really isn't the endeavour for you. You know the old saying, "if you love what you do, you'll never work a day in your life?" That was clearly made up by somebody that never ran a dog boarding business.

Again, I'm not trying to change your mind here. I want you to run a successful business, but I also want what is best for your and canine clients, though. If you're still with me, and are more determined than ever to run the most successful dog boarding business that you can, then I'm with you all the way!

With that mind, it's time to start thinking about the next step of your new career. Namely, what qualifications - if any - will you need to get the ball rolling on your business. Is it time to enrol in night school?

What Skills and Attributes are Required to Work with Dogs?

To run a successful dog boarding business, you'll need the following.

- A good working knowledge of dogs. You must understand the difference in temperaments, needs, behaviours and communication styles between a range of different canines. There is no such thing as a one-size-fits-all approach when it comes to dogs.
- An ability to diagnose basic medical issues in dogs, administering first aid where necessary and seeking urgent professional help if it's required. Dogs cannot tell you when

something is up. You'll need to work it out for yourself. I'll discuss canine healthcare and first aid in more detail in the pages to come.
- The patience and understanding required to communicate with dogs - and their human owners. That's right, you'll need to be both a dog person *and* a people person (hell, I know you were hoping to get away from people). Working for yourself doesn't mean that you lock yourself away in an ivory tower and stop interacting with anybody else.
- A willingness to learn. If you want to be successful, you'll need to stay up to date with the ever-changing legal landscape and needs of your canine clients. There will be plenty of courses out there that you can take. I'll discuss these throughout the course of this book.
- Bags of patience, and an unstinting sense of humour. When you're working with dogs, things can and will go wrong. After a while, you'll start to consider things going wrong to be the new normal. You'll need to be capable of expecting the unexpected, rolling with the tide, and various other clichés.

As you delve deeper in the pages of this book, you'll learn more and more about how to make your dog boarding business the best it can be. Before you do anything else, however, take another moment to consider whether you have the right personality for the job.

Is Your Plan to Run a Business from Your Home Legal?

There is one final elephant in the room that really needs to be taken into consideration. You need to ensure that your plans to run a business from your home are actually legally compliant.

I'm not talking about permits, laws surrounding animal care, and any other concerns. These are obviously critical, but I'll get to those in due course. First, you'll need to be certain that you're not breaking the law by running a business out of your home - period. Running a company is a very different beast to acting as a sole trader.

Before you go any further, make sure that you approach all the relevant authorities and utility suppliers and obtain permission to run a business from your home. These include:

- Your mortgage provider, or your landlord if you live in a rental property.
- Your local council.
- Your neighbours.
- Your insurance providers.
- Your telecommunications providers.

Let's take a look at each of these in a little more detail. This is important, so I hope that you're paying attention.

Mortgage Lenders

When you take out a mortgage, you'll be doing so on the principle that you're providing a family home. If you decide to turn it into a business premises, you may find yourself in contravention of the Ts and Cs of your mortgage.

That's not a good position to be in. If they're of a mind to do so, the mortgage lender can terminate your loan and demand repayment in full. If you can't meet that expectation, you'll be staring down the barrel of foreclosure and losing your home.

Before making any kind of decisions, speak to your mortgage lender. You may be able to obtain permission to use your home as a business site. Dig out the paperwork that you signed when you took out the mortgage and look for any loopholes. Above all, though, be honest and upfront. That will get you much further than trying to pull a fast one over on your mortgage provider.

If they say no, you have five options.

1) Ignore them. You won't bring it up again. But....
2) Stretch the truth and claim that your doggy business is a favour that you perform for friends and neighbours.
3) Appeal the decision and ask to escalate the issue further up the flagpole.
4) Transfer your mortgage to another provider that doesn't mind you running your business while indebted to them.
5) Give up your dream of a dog business and spiral into a hopeless funk of depression, cursing the fact that you wasted a small fortune on this book for no reason.

Personally, I don't recommend options 1 or 2. If something should happen to your home and you need to make an insurance claim, your mortgage provider will likely find out. If your business manages to annoy your neighbours (more on them in a moment), they may report you. This will not reflect well on you.

Naturally, we don't think that option 5 is the way to go, either. C'mon, you've come this far already! This leaves options 3 and 4 open to you. It sounds like a lot of work, but it will be worth it in the longer term.

It may also be in your best interests to look up your property on the Land Registry website. There could be restrictions placed on the site of your home that even a mortgage lender cannot control.

Landlords

If you rent your property, you are even more restricted than if you have a mortgage. You absolutely must notify your landlord of your intentions, and respect their right to say no. You'll be in all kinds of trouble if you plough on ahead without seeking permission in advance. If you lose your job and your business in quick succession, you're going to have a very bad day indeed.

Check your tenancy agreement and formulate a plan. Obviously if it says, "no pets" then you're onto a non-starter. You'll have to move, or appeal to the owner's better nature. It's hard to imagine they'll welcome countless dogs in the house if they refuse one, though.

The good news is that your landlord cannot withhold permission on grounds that would be dubbed unreasonable. The bad news is that a dog business provides a number of reasonable concerns. Your intentions may cause a great deal of wear and tear to the property, or if they feel that your clients will cause a nuisance to the neighbours.

Also, be prepared - the owner of the property will be well within their rights to expect a renegotiation of rental costs. It's similar to a mortgage agreement. You signed a contract for a residential agreement. If you're now running a business from the site, it's a different situation. This means that your existing agreement can be torn up, and a new one drawn up to reflect this change in circumstances.

Local Councils

If you plan to run a dog boarding business, you must inform the local council. This is because you'll need to apply for a licence. (Let’s ignore unscrupulous, illegally operating players who might be out there. These people don’t care if they eventually get prosecuted. Sadly, they do exist.) In addition, there may be logistical concerns that need to be taken into consideration.

Home improvements are an example. If you plan to run a business from your home, you may need to build an extension. Planning permission may be required for this. You may need planning permission without building work, too. It all depends on the policies of your particular local council. Naturally, you’ll need to investigate this. Even if this isn't the case, there will be logistics to think about that your council have strong views about. This includes parking and advertising.

Your local council could hit you with business rates to keep your company active from your property – it’s unlikely but worth checking. Just ensure your home and all its parts remain your home – not bits specifically for an office or dogs.

Another reason to notify your local authority is council tax. Running a business from your home may have an impact on this. Don't be surprised if your bill increases as a result. Again, this is something that you'll need to handle in advance. If your local authority discovers that you are running a business without notifying them, you may be on the hook for a fine.

Finally, if you live in a council-owned property, you will definitely need permission from the local authority. They will be acting as your landlord I n this instance. Again, in theory, this will not be a problem. In practice, though, the council may not be happy about the idea of your home being damaged by multiple dogs.

Neighbours

OK, I have mentioned the impact that your business may have on neighbours a number of times. There is a good reason for this. If your business is causing them a nuisance, your neighbours can complain and have your venture shut down.

Now, let's discuss the definition of a nuisance here. Don't panic if you live next door to an aspiring Victor Meldrew that seems to complain about everything and nothing. Simply being annoyed is not enough to carry any weight. To become a genuine nuisance, you will need to be actively impacting upon a neighbour's quality of life.

Examples of this include:

- Excessive Noise. If you have a house filled with dogs, you're doing to have a house filled with noise. Dogs love to wind each other up. If one starts barking, many more will follow. If your house has thin walls, this will obviously impact upon your neighbours. You may consider this appropriate revenge for the amount of noise their children make, but the law is unlikely to see it that way.
- Parking Spaces. You will have clients coming and going from your property to drop off and collect their canines. They may also come in to discuss the dog with you. If you share a driveway, and your clients are blocking access for your neighbours' car(s), they'll understandably have grounds to complain.
- Security. Your neighbours may object to you having a long and varied list of guests coming and going from your home. They may have a tough job convincing anybody that this is a sincere risk to their safety. It's possible though, especially if

there is any risk of the dogs in your care making their way into a neighbour's home via your back garden.

It pays to speak to your neighbours in advance about what you're planning and soften them up. They can take you to court if proof that you are causing a genuine nuisance, and a magistrate is likely to rule in their favour. CCTV could prove an incredibly worthwhile investment if ever evidence is required.

One way around annoying your neighbours could be to invest in a smart, aka silent, doorbell. These devices will not make a sound when somebody rings your bell. Instead, they'll flash LED lights or vibrate in your pocket. If you have countless deliveries and visitors coming and going, a silent doorbell will prevent a chorus of howling canines greeting every knock.

Insurers

Running a business – especially one that involves dogs – will clearly impact upon your insurance policies. You'll need to inform your home and contents insurer, for example. You will likely have taken out a policy that claims your home is a residential property, with a standard number of pets (if any.) A sizable number of animals in the home changes this.

I will discuss insurance in more detail elsewhere in this book. There is a wide range of policies that you should take out for your own protection. Before you reach this stage, however, make sure you'll be covered if you are running a business from your home.

Like everything we have discussed, there will likely be a cost implication to this. Expect your premiums to rise. You'll need to swallow this expense. It will prevent you from encountering any unpleasant surprises in the future.

Telecomms Suppliers

Seriously? What on earth does your broadband provider have to do with your decision to run a business from home? The service keeps dropping out while you're trying to Netflix and chill anyway. Surely what you do in the comfort of your own home is none of their business.

Well, the reality is, unless you took out a line for a business premises you'll be in breach of your contract. You will have been provided a price and line rental based on personal use. This means that your provider can pull the plug at a moment's notice, leaving you high and dry if they discover that you're using their services for work. You won't have access to the Internet – good luck running a business without that – and maybe even a phone line. What's more, you'll still have to pay up to settle any outstanding bills for your line rental.

Of course, you may believe that what your supplier doesn't know cannot possibly hurt them. That's true, to an extent. It can put you in something of a sticky situation, though. If something does go wrong with the service, you're going to struggle – you'll likely end up losing money as a result.

You'll doubtless want to complain. If you mention that you're running a business at this point, and demand your provider treats you as a priority for this reason, you'll be creating a rod for your own back.

For your own sake, it's best to front up when taking out a broadband or telephone connection. If you're halfway through a contract, call your provider and inform them of your change in circumstances. Sure, it may be more expensive. You can claim most of the bill as a tax-deductible expense, though.

If you've now established that a dog business is the right one for you, and you're not going to fall foul of the law in running such a venture, it's time to get started.

Chapter 3

Getting Started

If you haven't been deterred by what I've said so far, you're clearly ready to embark on your journey. Welcome in advance to the home boarding for dogs extended family. I'm thrilled to have you join this pack of professionals.

However, making the decision to get started is just the beginning. This is the point that you really need to start rolling up your sleeves and getting the ball rolling on your business. This chapter will be dedicated to getting started and preparing yourself for your new venture.

Before I start though, double- and triple-check that you have ticked all the legal boxes. Before you begin the process of applying for a license to run your business, ask yourself:

- Have you checked with, and informed, your mortgage broker or landlord that you plan to run a business from home?
- Have you informed your local authority, and confirmed that you will not require planning permission for your business?
- Have you informed all your utility and communications providers that you work from home, even though it retains its primary purpose as your domestic residence?
- Have you had a chat with your neighbours, discussed your intentions, and listened to any concerns they may have about your plans?
- Have you studied the relevant legislation surrounding your business plans, and know exactly what kind of license you'll need?

If you answered yes to all of these questions, it's time to contact your local authority and complete the necessary paperwork.

Applying for a License

Make an appointment with your local authority dog business licensing officer to discuss this. I've said before, and I'll say again – leave no stone unturned in your quest to obtain the appropriate license. Clear at least an hour of your schedule, and don't let the officer hurry you out of the door. You'll need to have a lengthy conversation, and don't assume anything.

There will be a charge for your license, and the cost varies between local authorities. You may also need to undergo a background check. Remember, your council can refuse to grant you a license if they see fit. Usually, this will only happen if you have previously been convicted of any kind of an animal welfare offense. If you are denied a license, you can appeal the decision at a Magistrate's Court.

Remember that your local authority may want to inspect your property before granting a license. A vet or another professional from the field of animal welfare will perform this inspection, so it's not just the local authority representative being a nosy busybody. Do not refuse or delay this inspection, or you'll just slow down your approval – and it could even be denied outright. The conditions of your license will be set according to the results of this inspection, including how many dogs you can take in at any given time.

Let's say, for example, that you own a house with three bedrooms, a living room, a kitchen, a bathroom, a utility room and a dining room. You have one dog of your own that lives with you, and a child aged ten. In this circumstance, you will likely be permitted to take in up to a maximum of 6 dogs at a time.

The thinking behind this is that, as per the regulations that I discussed in Chapter 1, every dog must have at least one room to call their own. A family bathroom can be counted. Your dog will also need to be assigned one of these rooms, and your ten-year-old child's bedroom will be disqualified. This leaves you with a potential 6 rooms left.

There will be other considerations as part of the inspection – most notably, the welfare of the dogs. Some local authorities (not in England) have adopted what is called the Lacors model home boarding guidance (e.g. Swansea council). This will cap all home boarders to a maximum of three dogs, regardless of the size of your property. I can't stress enough how important health and safety is here. I will discuss how you can dog-proof a home in just a moment. You will also be asked to prove that you can keep and maintain accurate records pertaining to your canine boarders, and what reasonable steps you will take to prevent outbreaks of contagious illness.

You will also need to prove that you can keep up with the physical demands on this line of work. You will be expected to provide most dogs with at least forty minutes of exercise each day, remember. If you do have a dog of your own, ensure it's looking bright-eyed and bushy-tailed when the inspector arrives. Anything you can do to make a good impression will work in your favour.

Your inspector may ask you to make changes or improvements to your home before agreeing to grant you a license. Again, if you disagree with these and consider them to be unfair or unreasonable, appeal to a Magistrate's Court. Try to remember that these people are animal welfare professionals, though. They have the best intentions of the dogs in mind, and enough experience to back up their beliefs. It may well pay to listen to them.

If your request for a license is approved and rubber-stamped, initially it will be valid for twelve months. Each year, you'll need to renew this and pay the relevant fees again. In theory, that will be that. You still have to undergo the process of being inspected every year and you will likely receive a spot check each year.

However, by law, your local authority can give notice of an inspection at any time. This will be done in writing, so they shouldn't just turn up at your door. If they do so without prior notification, just decline to let them enter unless it suits you. All the same, the prospect of this should be enough keep you on your toes. Your license can be suspended, or outright retracted, at any point.

If you make a start on your business and feel that you've made a mistake, a license can be transferred within the same local authority, if they agree. Perhaps you have a friend or family member that has expressed an interest in a similar venture, and they feel like they're more suited to this line of work. Your local authority will arrange this. Naturally, there will be a charge involved (when dealing with government bodies, there is *always* a charge involved), and whoever is requesting the license will need to demonstrate their suitability. If approved, the remaining time on the license will be transferred to this individual.

Getting Your Home Ready for Canine Boarders

As I have discussed, a big part of passing your inspection and gaining a license is proving that your home is safe and suitable for canine clients. This means that you're going to need to undertake a number of checks yourself. If an animal professional has any reason to suspect that the dogs under your care will not be safe, they'll have legitimate reason to reject your request for a boarding license.

Take a look around your home and look out for any potential hazards. Ensure that the dogs have access to an outside area without any interference. Above all, make sure that your home and garden are secure. Runaway dogs are never a good thing. This goes double when it's somebody else's pet, and you need to have an awkward conversation when an owner arrives to collect them.

Your primary concerns with making a home safe for dogs are:

Potential Toxins

Dogs are curious critters by their very nature. They have a sensational sense of smell, and in many cases, an insatiable hunger. This means that you'll need to make sure there is no chance of a dog in your care sniffing out, and accidentally consuming, a toxic substance.

Common foods and household items that are toxic to dogs include:

- Chocolate.
- Coffee, tea bags, and anything else with high caffeine content.
- Alcoholic beverages.
- Grapes, currants and raisins.
- Macadamia nuts.
- Onions and garlic.
- Human medications - including humble paracetamol.
- Cleaning products (bleach, window cleaner, oven cleaner, etc.)
- Antifreeze.
- Paint.

Keep all of these items way out of reach, ideally behind locked cabinet doors. I'll discuss what to do in the event of an emergency later in this book, but do everything in your power to prevent this from being necessary.

Potential Hazards

The dogs in your care will not only endangered by things they eat and drink. Obstacles and hazards that could fall on them are also a huge concern.

Always assume that the dogs in your care will clumsy oafs. *Adorable* clumsy oafs but lumbering buffoons all the same. Take a look around your home and look for things that could cause harm if knocked into or over.

That vase balanced on a thin table in the hall. That's got to go. It may look elegant now, but it won't when it falls on a dog's head after they nudge the table. Are you boarding at Christmastime? Factor dogs into your decorations. Trees and tinsel may become inadvertent health hazards. Make sure your windows aren't big enough for a dog to slip through, either.

When dealing with dogs, assume that whatever *can* be broken *will* be. Factor this into your home décor when preparing a dog boarding business (white carpets and sofas are a definite 'no no'), and keep the safety and security of your clients in mind at all times.

Time Out Zones

While dogs are social animals that rarely like to be alone, they can grow overwhelmed. This is especially likely if they are in a strange environment, surrounded by new dogs and an unfamiliar human. Every dog in your care will need somewhere they can go to be alone and re-centre their equilibrium.

This is why you'll need to ensure that you have a room for every dog in your house. Let them claim the room as their territory. That doesn't mean encouraging them to cock their leg and pee on the furniture. Just let them have a little sniff around, and maybe a roll on the rug.

It will also help the dog feel at home if you ask for something from their home. A blanket that they sleep on, or an item of clothing worn by an owner. Dogs are guided by their nose. If there's a familiar scent in a particular location, they'll feel much more comfortable there.

Feeding and Water Areas

Feeding time is the highlight of many doggy days (aside from walkies, a treat, playtime, and ... let's face it, a dog's life is one long highlight reel). However, some dogs have a complicated relationship with food.

The dogs in your care will have attended puppy training if they have responsible owners, but dogs don't attend pre-school. This means that sharing is not ingrained into their psyche. In fact, some dogs become positively devilish if another pooch attempts to take a nibble from their food bowl.

To offset the risk of food aggression, it's advisable to feed all dogs in your care separately. Use those timeout zones that we have just discussed. The dogs can eat in peace, and then re-join the pack afterwards with a full tummy and head filled with happy thoughts. Your license obliges you to actively take this approach. At the very least, you must ensure you have a dog owner's consent to feed their dog in the company of another.

Hygienic Bathroom Areas

If you're lucky, the dogs in your care will save up all their bodily functions for walkies. It's likely, however, that they'll need to relieve themselves on your property from time to time. It's highly advisable to set up a designated toilet spot for all your canine clients.

The good news is that this will be comparatively simple to do. Pick a spot in the garden and consider fencing it off with a gate for access.

This means the dogs will soon come to realise what this particular area is for.

Spray a urine-encouraging scent on this patch of grass to get the ball rolling. Alternatively, if you have a dog of your own, train them to this use this spot. Dogs like to urinate in the same place as each other. It's how they establish that they are a pack – it's sending a message to rival canines that says, "mess with one of us and you mess with all of us."

Access to the Garden

One of the most important rules in dog boarding regulations is that the canines have access to an outside area. As we've just discussed, they'll use this to do their business. In addition, the dogs may want to play in the garden, or even just bask in the sunshine. Dogs don't produce Vitamin D organically, so they like to absorb it from the natural rays of the sun.

You'll have to limit time outside to prevent the dogs from developing heatstroke, or any similar complaint. Likewise though, you won't want to be up and down letting them in and out every time they express a whim.

The easiest way to do this is to build or invest in a dog flap. If you're worried about security, get a flap that's activated by collar microchips. These are designed for cats, but you should be able to find something that's appropriate for canines.

Security in the Garden

Once the dogs are in the garden, you also need to make sure that they don't get out again. Fences are an absolute must if you don't want the dogs inviting themselves into your neighbour's property.

In addition, you'll also need to look at potential garden hazards. Do you have a pond, or a swimming pool? If so, keep them covered. Just because dogs can swim, it doesn't mean that they'll be safe falling into such water. The temperature change could put them in shock, or they could swallow excessive water. Chlorine and other cleaning chemicals could also spark a nasty reaction on your dog's skin.

Think about your plants, too. The dogs will spend a disproportionate amount of time sniffing around the garden. When a smell tickles their fancy, the next action of most dogs will be to see what it tastes like.

The Kennel Club lists the following plants as being toxic to canines:

- Aconitum
- Amaryllis bulbs
- Asparagus fern
- Azalea
- Cyclamen
- Daffodil bulbs
- Day lilies
- Delphiniums
- Foxgloves
- Hemlock
- Hyacinth
- Hydrangea
- Ivy
- Laburnum
- Lily of the valley
- Lupins
- Morning glory
- Nightshade
- Oleander
- Rhododendron
- Rhubarb leaves
- Sweet pea
- Tulip bulbs
- Umbrella plant
- Wisteria
- Yew

If you grow any of these in your garden, get them removed as quickly as possible.

Children

On paper, running a dog business when you have children is a match made in heaven. Many children love dogs. Many dogs, in return, love children. Your kids and your clients will contentedly play together in the garden, exhausting each other, and you can sit back with a well-earned cup of tea and watch.

Sadly, the reality doesn't always match up to the theory. In fact, you may even be refused a boarding license if you live with young children under the age of 5. Kids and canines can often wind each other up, and the results can be dangerous. A young child that does not understand boundaries might try to ride a large dog like a pony, yank a poor pooches tail to get their attention, or even poke a dog in the eye. Young children do not always pick up on a dog's subtle cues when they suggest they've had enough.

On the other side of the coin, dogs do not always understand their own strength. The canines in your care may start jumping and roughhousing. This will scare the living daylights out of your child at best, and injure them at worst. If a child retaliates on instinct, things could quickly get ugly. The situation will go from bad to worse if other members of the dog's pack decide to back up their buddy.

If any person aged under 16 years resides at the home, there must be procedures in place to regulate the interactions between the dogs and that person.

You will need to undertake a risk assessment and have a policy in place for any other children under 16 entering your premises.

Think long and hard about whether your family dynamic is suitable for dogs. if you decide to go ahead, and you're permitted to do so, set some very specific rules for your children about how they can and cannot interact with your canine houseguests.

Yes, parents will always want to put their children's wishes first. However, you need to remember that you're running a business and taking money from pet owners. This means that the customer is always right.

Other Pets

Finally, think about any other pets that you have in your home. A goldfish in your kid's bedroom is unlikely to cause a problem. A cat, however, can make for an uneasy housemate.

England's regulations, for example, are very specific. "It is not recommended that cats are resident on the premises if dogs are being home boarded. If there are resident cats, the licence holder must identify potential stressors to the cat/s and demonstrate how these would be mitigated in order to protect the cats' welfare." (DEFRA - The Animal Welfare (Licensing of Activities Involving Animals) (England) Regulations 2018 - Guidance notes for conditions for providing home boarding for dogs November 2018).

Insurance Policies That You're Going to Need

Back in the previous chapter, I discussed the importance of informing your home insurer that you are opening your home to dogs. I'll stress again that you *must* do this. If you don't, you'll likely find that your policy is declared null and void and you will be paying a monthly fee for nothing. You probably won't discover this until you try – and fail – to make a claim, though.

In addition to home insurance, there are other policies that you must take out before starting your business. Yes, it's more expense.

Hopefully it will be a needless expense that you never need to make use of. If you do find yourself in a sticky situation, however, being appropriately insured will make all the difference.

Let's take a look at some of the policies that will set your mind at rest, and help you sleep better at night. Most of these are not legal requirements, but that doesn't mean that you should skip them. Policies to consider taking out include:

- Public Liability Insurance.
- Small Business Insurance.
- Employer's Liability Insurance.
- Income Protection Insurance.
- HMRC Audit Insurance.

Let's take a look at each of these policies in a little more detail.

Public Liability Insurance

If you only take out one additional insurance policy, protecting your public liability is an imperative for your licence. This policy will shield you against a range of mishaps that could occur while the dogs are in your care, or while you're out walking them. There are a range of different circumstances where you'll be glad that you a public liability insurance policy in place.

This policy will cover any expenses incurred if one of the dogs in your care is injured, or a member of the public is hurt as a result of your occupation. Here are some examples of situations whereby you may need to call upon this level of protection.

- You're out walking the dogs. You have an extendable lead, and one of the pooches decides to take advantage of this. They take a further unsanctioned stroll, and a member of the public trips over the lead and hurts themselves. By the letter of the law, this mishap was your fault and you could face civil action for any medical bills or loss of earnings.
- One of your clients asks you to drop a dog off at their home. They give you a key, and trust you to let yourself in. So far, so good – but you forget to lock the door properly on the way out, and the client is burgled as a result. Alternatively, you could knock over a priceless vase in the home. Your insurance policy will prevent you from needing to personally reimburse your client.
- Your neighbour takes in a package for you while you were out walking the dogs. They come over to drop the package off, and one of the dogs has a mad moment and bites your neighbour, or knocks them off their feet with an enthusiastic greeting. Again, as the dogs were in your care, you'll be

responsible for their behaviour. Insurance will cover any financial penalties you'll be liable for.

- One of the dogs in your care manages to escape your attention and gets themselves into mischief somewhere in the home. Maybe they eat something they shouldn't and make themselves unwell. Maybe they get into a fight with another pet. Maybe they find themselves in the kitchen and cut their paw on a knife that you forgot to put away. Any of these scenarios will result in a trip to the vet, and associated bills, as well as any damages for the emotional trauma inflicted upon the dog. Having the right insurance policy will help you cover these costs.

Some companies will offer a policy called Pet Boarding Insurance. As the name suggests, this policy will be tailored for your particular needs – and it will also include Public Liability Insurance. This is something that is well worth looking into.

Small Business Insurance

Small Business Insurance will cover the majority of the situations that I described above, under the cover of Public Liability Insurance. If something goes wrong while you're working – and accidents *will* happen, especially when you're working with dogs – you'll be granted a measure of protection. The monthly fee of your policy will be considerably smaller than any payments that you're liable for.

In addition, Small Business Insurance may pay out for damage to your property if your Home Insurance policy declines to help, even if the issue is not directly related to dogs.

Your home could be damaged by flooding, for example, after a period of heavy rainfall. If your Home Insurance policy considers this to be an act of nature and thus not applicable for a payment, your Small Business Insurance may think otherwise as your home is also your place of work. It's an extra layer of protection that will help you sleep a little easier at night.

If your business is being investigated due to a Pubic Liability claim, you may also find that you're temporarily unable to work. You certainly may not be able to maintain the same volume of clients and workload until the situation is resolved. A Small Business Insurance policy may be able to keep your business afloat during this difficult time, until you can get back on your feet.

Employer's Liability Insurance

If your business starts to grow, you may need to bring in additional support in the form of employees.

This could be assistant dog walker for when you don't have time to exercise the dogs yourself. It could be a second pair of hands around the home, pitching in with general support. It could even be something as simple as a driver, escorting you or your canine clients to other homes to collect or drop off doggies before and after their day of boarding.

The reality is, if you employ *anybody* for your business and pay a salary, you are legally required to take out Employer's Liability Insurance. This means that you'll be able to continue to pay the staff member if they become sick or injured as a direct result of working for you.

With dogs, there will always be the risk of personal injury. Your employee could slip and fall while on a dog walk, twisting their ankle and being unable to work for a while. They may be bitten by a dog and experience some nasty side effects, such as infection around the puncture site. They could even slip and fall on your staircase, or on a wet floor because you cleaned the kitchen that morning.

Whatever the explanation, you'll be liable for this staff member's earnings while they can't make money themselves. In addition, you'll likely have to pay out a second salary for a temporary replacement to ensure the work gets done. Employer's Liability Insurance means that you'll be able to make these payments without devastating the bottom line of your business.

Income Protection Insurance

If you work alone, you won't need to worry about staff being unable to perform their duties. All the mishaps that could befall a staff member could also apply to you, though. If you run your own business, illness and injury can be catastrophic. If you can't work, you cannot earn money. This could lead to difficulty paying your rent or mortgage, and other bills. Savings only go so far.

In addition, stop to think about what you'll do if something were to happen to your partner, child or parent. You could unexpectedly find yourself in a position where you need to dedicate yourself to being a full-time carer on a temporary basis. This, again, will have a big impact on your business plans. It's easy to plan for the future when everything is running smoothly. It automatically becomes much harder when you're unable to meet your commitments.

If you take out a Personal Income Insurance policy, you'll be protected in the event of being unable to work. How much you have to spend depends on how much you'll expect as a monthly payment from your insurer. It's advisable to take out a policy that covers your rent or mortgage, at the very least. Failing to protect yourself will make an already stressful situation considerably worse for you.

Just check the small print and ensure that you're taking out a policy that will offer a shield to your unique circumstances. If necessary, look into a separate policy for serious or critical illness cover.

HMRC Audit Insurance

The last policy that I'll discuss is very much optional, but like so many other policies, it could save you some real headaches down the line. HMRC have the right to audit your business if they see fit, and it's not a fun experience. The audit can take in excess of a year, and usually costs a small fortune in accountancy fees.

In addition, you'll be responsible for a lot of the work yourself. This will take your attention away from your business. Throw in the sleepless nights caused by the stress of being audited (HMRC do not have a reputation for being fluffy and understanding about perceived financial irregularities) and you have a potential nightmare on your hands.

Common reasons why HMRC may decide to audit your business include:

- They've been tipped off about potential tax fraud. Anybody can make this accusation – disgruntled former employees, neighbours with a grudge, or a rival business owner. It's not necessarily likely, and HMRC may ignore the suggestion, but you'll certainly appear on their radar if you are referred as a person of interest.
- You make regular errors on your tax returns. Mistakes happen, and tax returns are complicated. Making errors each and every time, however, will rouse suspicion – especially if you regularly report earnings below the correct threshold, or overestimate your deductible expenses.
- Your returns vary wildly year-on-year. HMRC will expect to see your earnings grow over time. They will likely understand how you could experience a sudden spike from year one to year two. If your earnings drop sharply, though? That will raise eyebrows. There will likely be a good reason for this, but ensure that the tax authorities are aware of it.
- Your business will also rouse suspicion if you are reporting lower earnings that the industry standard. Obviously every business will report different numbers. It depends on your pricing structure, how many dogs you take in, and how many hours you decide to work. HMRC will have an idea of what a dog boarding business should bring in, though. If you constantly claim that your profits are below a taxable

threshold, they may start to wonder if you're strictly on the up-and-up.
- You’re in the wrong place at a wrong time. Sometimes, a HMRC audit is just bad luck. They may decide to audit your business at random.

If you take out a HMRC Audit Insurance policy, you'll be financially protected while the audit takes place. It will not prevent the audit from happening, and it won't speed up the end result, but at least any fees incurred will be taken care of.

These expenses could run to north of £5,000, so protection is advisable. In addition, many insurers that offer these policies will also offer dedicated help and advice throughout the process. You will have somebody in your corner that understands what is happening and works with you every step of the way. This will make the experience considerably less stressful.

Courses to Take

Before opening your doors and registering a business, I also recommend taking some courses. Education is critical, and the more you know, the better positioned you’ll be when it comes to handling your canine clients.

It’s up to you whether you take all of the courses that we’re about to discuss. I strongly recommend that you take a doggy first aid course and get certificated at the very least. Just because you have insurance, it doesn’t mean that you can play hard and fast with the welfare of your canine clients.

In addition, remember that qualifications are never a negative selling point. If you can prove that you have taken the appropriate steps to learn about your chosen business, your license application will run much smoother.

Customers will also be assured by accreditation. If you were hiring a babysitter for your toddler and had two choices, one of whom was enthusiastic but had no formal education and another that studied childcare at college or University, which would you choose?

Courses to consider include:

- An OFQUAL regulated Level 2 qualification (e.g. Level 2 Diploma in Animal Care)
- An OFQUAL regulated Level 3 qualification (e.g. A Level 3 Award in Canine Care, Behaviour and Welfare – or a similar approved course that embraces this and Professional Boarding and Day Care.)

- Dog handling/basic training course
- OFQUAL regulated Level 2 City & Guilds Technical Competence in Dog Walking
- NARPS Dog Walking and Pet Sitting Diploma
- Canine First Aid.
- Pet Bereavement.

You can take many of these courses from the comfort of your own home online or find a local provider. The latter is obviously preferable, as this will ensure that you gain hands-on experience with a dog in tow. Alternatively, take a mix-and-match approach. Now, let's take a look at these courses in more detail.

England's licensing regulations for example specify that, "training must be a minimum of an OFQUAL regulated level 2 qualification in a relevant subject, or clear evidence of knowledge and experience."

Level 3 Award in Canine Care, Behaviour and Welfare

This Award is regulated by OFQUAL, the Office of Qualifications and Examinations Regulation. That's right – its government sponsored-accreditation. This means that it's very thorough and will have a price tag to match. It will also take quite some time to complete in its entirety.

The OFQUAL Level 3 is a mandatory requirement for England's 'Higher Standard' criteria for a Home Boarding business

You may prefer a cheaper alternative, such as a general Pet Sitting Course. If you find a course that is tailored to running a business, this may be suitable. You will learn the basics about canine care, in addition to gaining insights into running a business.

It's advisable to combine such a course with some additional learning, though. Having a top line understanding of several subjects is admirable, but you'll really flourish if you can call yourself an expert.

Dog Obedience Classes

Dogs are wonderful animals, but they can also be strong-willed at times. Give a dog an inch, and they'll likely take a mile – then turn around offer a huge grin that melts your heart, knowing that they're handsome enough to get away with mischief-making.

If you take a course on basic dog obedience, you will enjoy a greater control over the dogs in your care. This will be essential, as you'll need to know that the animals will respond to your voice commands. You can't be everywhere, at all times. There will be occasions that you'll be relying on a dog respecting your authority from afar. You'll also learn how to forge a connection to the dogs in your care. You want your canine clients to behave because through a desire to please you, not because they're afraid of getting into trouble.

By taking obedience classes, you'll gain a better understanding of how different breeds of dog communicate. There can be a world of difference between instructing a Shih Tzu and an Alsatian, after all. When you also consider that every canine is born with a unique personality, you'll have plenty to think about. If possible, borrow dogs of differing shapes and sizes from friends and family and take them to classes to gain first-hand insight.

Just be careful not to mix up obedience with discipline. If a dog steps out of line, you'll need to set up very strict parameters with your human clients about how to manage doggy misbehaviour. I'll cover this in more detail in our next chapter, in which I'll discuss policies.

Certification in Dog Walking

A course on dog walking may sound money for old rope. You attach a lead, take a stroll, and maybe throw a tennis ball around. How on earth could this require certification?

The fact is, dog walking – especially when you take out multiple canines at the same time – can be a tricky experience. I'll discuss the many trials and tribulations that dog walkers will encounter throughout their days elsewhere in this book. By taking an accredited course, however, you'll have first-hand experience of how to deal with issues.

You will also learn more about canine anatomy during this course. Varying breeds of dog have different bone structures, and if you're not careful, you could inadvertently leave a canine at risk of arthritis.

Small dogs, for example, have to work hard to keep up with their larger counterparts. Bigger breeds, however, come with their own challenges. If you know how to keep all the dogs in your care happy and healthy, you'll enjoy a more successful business.

Canine First Aid

OK, this is the course that I'm not prepared to budge on. If you have dogs in your home, you *must* have first aid accreditation so you can handle any mishaps. Fingers crossed you'll never need to put your training into practice. If you do, however, rushing to a vet is not always an option.

By learning canine first aid, you'll be able to act as a first line of treatment against cuts and bleeding, accidents involving electricity and hot surfaces, and what to do if the dog is stung or bitten by an insect or snake. You'll also gain a familiarity in how to handle heatstroke or hypothermia.

I'm going to discuss first aid and the physical well-being of dogs throughout this book. Even so, no matter how much detail we go into, we will insist on doggy first aid accreditation. You'll likely find that your human clients are just as adamant as we are.

Pet Bereavement

This qualification will very much be a case of added value. However, it may help you process any future heartbreak, in addition to offering support to your human clients that have lost a treasured canine companion.

Gaining a professional understanding into the process of pet bereavement will not make you a qualified counsellor. Neither should you aim for it to do so. Striking a balance between an emotional attachment to the dogs that you care for and maintaining professional boundaries is a very fine line, and it can feel like a struggle to walk at times.

You'll learn how to manage the other dogs in your care though, who may be pining for their lost associate. It's believed that dogs have a basic understanding of death, but there are limits to their comprehension. If a dog is present every day for years, and is suddenly absent, it will create feelings of unrest and insecurity.

In addition, you will be able to offer advice on the practical side of pet bereavement. You'll have a wealth of knowledge about ceremonial proceedings, and how best to move forward in a new life without a cherished companion.

Do not attempt to absorb the grief of your human clients. That's not your job. Being able to offer an empathetic support network, however, will endear you a great deal. After all, if you can't be expected to understand the pain of losing a dog, who can?

How Much is All of This Going to Cost?

How long is a piece of string? It depends on how many improvements your home will need, and which part of the UK you are based in. As you can imagine, work on your home likely costs more in London than it would in, say, East Yorkshire.

You should also shop around for your insurance policies. Price comparison sites are a great place to start, but always schedule a one-on-one conversation with a broker. Dog business insurance is a specialised niche. You'll need to ensure that your particular needs will be met by your policy. Paying a monthly fee to an insurer that will not help you out when you need them most is the very definition of wasting money.

Courses will also vary in expense. Do your homework and find a vendor that combines the appropriate accreditation with value for money. Don't just assume that the most expensive option is the best. The Internet, in particular, is home to a number of opportunistic individuals that are keen to turn a fast buck. Look for reviews and seek out dog business support communities on social media.

Sit down and do some sums before you start your business, and confirm that your plans are economically viable. Conventional wisdom dictates that it could take as long as two to three years for a business to become profitable, so factor this into your considerations.

With the right dedication and promotion, you will likely be able to buck this trend. Protect yourself, and your family, by thinking things through. Speculating to accumulate is great, but only if you actually manage to turn a profit.

Do check out the web link I provide at the end of this book called 'Helpful Links' for a number of useful pointers.

Registering Your Business

There is no need to register as a limited company. You can enjoy a successful business career as a sole trader. Just register online with HMRC, which only takes a few minutes.

Just remember – the moment you register, you are on HMRC's radar. You'll be provided with a Taxpayer Identification Number, or TIN. This means that you'll be liable for filing an annual tax return by the end of every January. You'll also need to pay taxes twice a year. I'll discuss tax in more detail in the next chapter of this book.

You can earn up to £85,000 per annum – after expenses – before you need to consider charging your clients VAT. There's nothing to say that you're unable to do so earlier, if that's your wish.

Limited Company vs. Sole Trader – What's the Difference?

The biggest difference between operating as a company and a sole trader is liability. As a sole trader, you are personally liable for everything connected to your work. Financial filing and reporting, personal mishaps and injuries, violation of the law – this all falls on your head as an individual. This is why it's so important to keep your insurance policies up to date.

If you register as a limited company, there is a degree of separation between yourself and your business. The responsibility falls on Joe's Dog Boarding Ltd, not Joe Bloggs the individual. Third parties and suppliers may also happier to deal with a limited company. Perception is reality, and some people perceive a limited company to be more professional than a sole trader.

Setting up a limited company makes more work for yourself, though. You'll need to register through Companies House. There is a fee attached to this. At the time of writing, it's £12 to register online and £40 to register by post.

Once your company is registered, you can no longer complete self-assessment tax returns. You are now on the hook to submit business accounts once a year – accounts which can be viewed by the public upon request. You'll probably want to hire an accountant to help with this. That's another expense, but it will work out a lot cheaper – and considerably less stressful – than paying HMRC fines for mistakes and delays.

Chapter 4

Tax, Employee and Pension Considerations

Tax is nobody's idea of a fun subject. In truth though, tax implications should be taken very seriously when weighing up starting a business. There a multitude of options open to you. Some of them will potentially save money, and others will possibly cost more.

Ensure that you know what you're letting yourself in for. Many small business owners have been caught out by a failure to prepare appropriately for tax repayments. Healthy profit margins can look very different once HMRC have taken their share, and there is little wriggle room if you're not ready to pay your bill in full and on-time.

Before I go any further, we need to do a little housekeeping. Please read the below and take it very seriously. This is important.

- Nobody affiliated with this book is a tax expert, an accountant, lawyer or affiliated with the HMRC in any way. Treat this chapter as guidance based on personal experience, not legally binding financial advice.
- Tax law changes all the time. Everything you read here is correct to the best of our knowledge, at the time of writing. There may be adjustments made at any time, however. If in doubt, consult HMRC or an accountant.

Hopefully that makes things clear. There's no need to skip this chapter. The data I'll provide will put some helpful information into plain English, and get the ball rolling for your tax-based considerations. I cannot stress enough that we are not professionals in this field, though. The argument, "but *Randle* said that this was fine!" will not hold any water with HMRC.

Tax Implications as a Sole Trader

On paper, tax as a sole trader is a simple equation. At the end of every financial year, you hand over 20% of your earnings to HMRC and move on with your life. Job done?

No so. While it's true that being a sole trader – and filling in a self-employment tax return – is less complex than business accounts, you'll still need to factor a number of things into your thinking. You may find that registering as a limited company will save you money on your tax bill.

Here are a few basic facts to get the ball rolling.

- From the moment you register as self-employed with HMRC, you are liable for tax repayments.
- You can register at any time up two years from the start of your trading date. Your tax repayments will be back-dated, though.
- The tax year runs from April 6 to April 5. If you file your tax return by post, this must be completed by October. If you do so online, it must be completed by the following January. For example, if you trade between 6th April 2020 and 5th April 2021, you must file your tax return by 31st October 2021 (post) or 31st January 2022 (online.)
- If you fail to file your tax return on time, you'll be hit with an automatic fine of £100. This will increase if three months pass without filing the return. You'll also be charged interest on any late repayments, and there may be further fixed penalties involved.

Now let's dig a little deeper into the nitty-gritty and shed some light on what you may be expected to actually pay.

- Your first £12,500 of profit will be tax-free. This is called your personal allowance. If you earned less than £12,500, you'll still need to file a tax return. You just won't have to pay any income tax.
- Tax repayments are due on the *profits* of your business, not your total earnings. In other words, you pay tax on your net turnaround, not gross. If you made £40,000 over the year but incurred £5,000 of allowable expenses, your taxable profits would total £22,500.
- Tax is charged at a rate of 20% for profits between £12,501 and £49,999. If you earn £50,000 or more, you'll pay a tax rate of 40%.
- In addition to tax for the previous year, you'll need to pay an additional 50% of your bill toward the following year's return. You will then pay another 50% by the end of July. These are known as balancing payments. Don't be caught out by this the first time you file a tax return. Always be prepared to pay 150% of your anticipated tax.

With us so far? Well, there's more. In addition to tax, you'll need to pay into two National Insurance accounts. These charges will be added to your bill when the final calculation is made.

- National Insurance 2 is payable at a rate of £3 per week on all profits above £6,365. If you earn less than £6,365, you'll be given the option to pay this voluntarily.
- National Insurance 4 is charged at a rate of 9% on all profits between £8,632 and £50,000. This rate drops to 2% after the £50,000 threshold is reached.

Once you fill in your tax return, you will be told exactly what you owe for the year. If you think you're going to struggle to pay on time, get in touch with HMRC. It won't be a fun conversation, but it's a critical one. You may be able to set up a payment plan or be given an extension.

Oftentimes, no further action will be taken if you can commit to repaying in full on a particular date. Just ignoring the problem and hoping it will go away may cost you your business, however. The fines can add up, and the debt may be sold to a third party. Would you leave your dog with somebody that is battling with bailiffs at their front door?

Tax Implications of a Limited Company

An alternative to operating as a sole trader is setting yourself up as a limited company. Personally, I wouldn't recommend this unless you are turning over some serious income over the course of the year. However, once your reach a certain point of profitability, you can pay less tax by setting up a limited company.

On paper, the tax implications of a limited company are simple. Your business will pay a 19% corporate tax rate on all profitable income. The tax return can be complex here though, so you're advised to hire an accountant to help.

Naturally, as the owner of a limited company, you'll still need to pay NI contributions and income tax. Does this mean that you'll be taxed twice? Not necessarily. There are ways to juggle the numbers and ensure that you are not liable for personal taxes. You can even keep below the NI threshold while still maintaining access to a state pension.

If all this sounds illegal, it isn't. If it sounds unethical ...well, that's between you and your conscience. I'm talking loopholes here, and loopholes can be exploited by those with the knowledge and inclination to do so. That's a job for professional accountants, and that's who you should discuss these matters with. I will say no more about it here.

If you reach turnover over £45k PA, you should consider looking into registering as a limited company. You may be able to save yourself some serious money. If you reach £85k on turnover, you should *really* file as a company. At this point, you are legally obligated to become VAT-registered.

Once you're registered for VAT, you are obligated to apply an additional 20% to the value of any invoices that you issue to your clients. You can reclaim any VAT that you pay on goods and services, though.

Again, VAT is a complicated subject that's best left to professionals. By the time you're eligible to pay – and charge – this tax, you should have a full-time accountant on your books. By this stage, errors and mishaps with HMRC will become extremely costly and serious.

Tax-Deductible Expenses

As discussed, tax is only payable on the profits of your business. This means that you deduct expenses before HMRC works out how much money you owe them. Keep receipts for anything related to your business if you feel you'll be able to deduct them from your tax return. You won't need to upload them as part of your tax return, but HMRC may ask to see them after the event.

Naturally, the government is pretty strict about what constitutes a business expense. There is also plenty of misinformation out there surrounding this subject. Do not push your luck when claiming expenses on your tax return. That's a quick way to raise suspicion and get audited, which is an expensive and stressful experience.

Typically, a self-employed person can claim the following expenses against their tax return.

- **Stationery**. If you purchase any stationery for your business – toner cartridges for a printer, pens and pencils for an office, paper for printing off invoices and contracts, etc – you can claim this back.
- **Printing Costs**. Alternatively, you may decide to use a professional printing service to run off flyers and the like. This is considered an acceptable expense, provided it's within reason.
- **Insurance Costs**. Your professional insurance policies are considered a business expense. There really is no excuse not to take these out.
- **Professional Services**. If you hire an accountant to help with your taxes, their services are tax-deductible. Ain't life grand? This also applies to payroll software, and additional help that you may need to call upon.

- **Salaries and Pension Contributions for Staff**. If you have employees, the expenses incurred by paying salaries and contributing to a pension can be removed from your tax return.

Never mind all of that, though. You're running a dog boarding business. You want to know if the costs directly associated with the welfare of your canine clients are tax-deductible.

Happily, the answer is yes. You'll be able to claim back the cost of food, leads, muzzles, harnesses and any emergency vet bills. Just remember, these may be queried. Make sure that you can back up everything that you claim. Don't slip some gourmet treats for your own pet in with your expenses, or write off the bill for your own dog to have his teeth cleaned. If you're found out, there will be consequences.

Home and travel expenses are a little more complicated. You'll be working from home, so you'll be entitled to make an expense claim. You can't just reclaim your entire rent or mortgage payments, though. HMRC permit a sliding scale, known as the simplified payment structure, based on how many hours you spend working.

- If you work from 25 to 50 hours a month, you can claim £10 for every month.
- If you work from 51 to 100 hours a month, you can claim £18 for every month.
- If you work from over 100 hours a month, you can claim £26 for every month.

Vehicle expenses have a similar simplified structure. You may agree to collect and drop off your canine clients from and to their home addresses. You may also drive to a good spot for walkies. You can claim 45p per mile for the first 10,000 miles you cover as part of your business. After this, the rate drops to 25p per mile. Again though, you're in murky waters if you start mixing personal errands with your business drives. Don't take a 30-mile detour to your favourite shopping centre and try to squeeze it onto the same clam.

You're welcome to attempt to claim back a portion of your other household expenses, such as broadband, gas and electricity. You'll need to provide a home that's an appropriate temperature for dogs, and it's impossible to run a successful business without internet access. You'll expected to break down the costs fairly between personal and professional use, though.

When the time comes to fill in your tax return, you'll be asked to enter your expenses. The sum total will automatically be removed from your payable tax. So, if you've earned £40,000 and have £5,000 of expenses, your taxable profit will break down as follows:

£40,000 - £12,500 (personal allowance) - £5,000 (expenses) = £22,500 tax payable.

This would lead to a tax bill of roughly £8,150. That breaks down as:

- £4,500 (20% of the taxable profit)
- £2,250 (additional 50% balancing payment)
- £150 (NI2 contributions)
- £1,250 (NI4 contributions)

An additional £2,250 will also be due by July of the following year.

Are you starting to see how important expenses are? You will want to get that bill down as much as you possibly can. Just keep it legal and ethical.

Taking on Employees

As your business starts to grow, you may wish to take on additional help. Just some of the things that you may outsource include:

- Dog walking.
- Dog obedience training.
- General dogsitting while you run errands.
- Doggy playtime.

First thing's first. Know the difference between employees and workers. Employees enjoy more formal perks and benefits than workers. The distinction is a little unclear, so it's best to check with a professional as to what category your hired help falls into.

In essence, a worker is essentially somebody that performs tasks for you on the equivalent of a zero-hour contract. There is no obligation that you will need them at set times each day or week. Workers are also free to seek employment with other people and decline any offers of work that you make them. You have no legal right to the time, expertise or experience of a worker. If you have an unstinting schedule in place, you're more likely looking at an employee situation. A worker also cannot be expected to provide their services for more than 48 hours on any given week, unless they give written notice that they are prepared to opt out of this legal right.

In addition, workers cannot have any influence over your business. They must not be permitted to make decisions that could have business implications. They must not be indispensable in any way. If you hire somebody to help you out because they have a particular skill or qualification, and you struggle to get by without them, they will usually be considered an employee.

A short-term freelancer or contractor could also be considered a worker. This is rare, though – if you're taking somebody on for the duration of a contract, you'll likely have agreements in place as to when and how they'll be working for you. Even contractors have the legal right to be treated as employees if they are playing a pivotal role in your business. The law is weighted toward protecting the rights of employees. Always bear this in mind before taking on additional help. You will need to pay them holiday, sick pay and provide mandatory rest breaks.

Whether you have an employee or a worker helping you out, they are entitled to paid holiday. The government mandate is 5.6 weeks of holiday per year – pro rata. That is based upon a 5-day, 37.5-hour working week. You can reduce this entitlement if they work fewer hours. Speak to a legal professional about this. You should also seek advice on how to approach bank holidays, observance of religious holidays and sickness pay.

they'll need to be paid the national living wage. This varies by age.

- **Under 18 –** £4.35 per hour.
- **18 – 20 years –** £6.15 per hour.
- **21 – 24 years –** £7.70 per hour.
- **25 years or older –** £8.21 per hour.

Don't make the mistake of thinking that because nobody has signed a contract your relationship is strictly casual, either. Under UK law, a contract is not required to cement a working relationship. You will, however, be expected to put the following data in writing. An email will do.

- Your name and address – and company name, if applicable.
- The employee's job title, and a short description of their expected tasks.
- A start date of when they began working for you.
- Confirmation of expected hours of work.
- Acknowledgement of their salary, and legal rights to holiday and sick pay.
- Advice on how to react in the event of grievance against you, their employer.

- Confirmation of any mutual notice period should either of you choose to terminate your working relationship.

You must have an Employers' Liability (EL) insurance policy, valued at a minimum of £5million, in place if you take on employees. If you are asked to present evidence of this policy and fail to do so, you can be fined £1,000. If evidence if found that you are employing people without this policy in place, the fine rises to £2,500.

The good news is that you're not liable for your employee's tax status or returns. If they fail to register with HMRC, or do not pay their bill, you are not responsible for their actions. Just be prepared to be asked awkward questions if the individual comes under investigation. You may be asked to provide evidence of your working relationship, and even come under audit yourself.

Pensions

The final consideration that you'll need to make is your pension – and that of anybody that works for you.

As a business owner or a sole trader, you won't have an employer paying into a private pension for you. You'll still be entitled to your state pension once you reach an appropriate age. This will be paid at a rate proportionate to what you paid into it, through contributions. Will this be enough to sustain you through your dotage?

Speak to a pension advisor and discuss your options surrounding a private arrangement. It's advisable to at least know your options. If you would rather not have a pension, you could look into an ISA or similar savings account. You will be entitled to save up to £20,000 in such a way each year without any tax implications.

As an employer, you'll need to automatically enrol anybody that works for you into a pension scheme. This is law, under the Pensions Act of 2008. There are only two exceptions to this rule:

- The employee is younger than 22, or older than the state pension age.
- The employee earns less than £10,000 per year/£833 per month/£192 per week (pre-tax.)

In these instances, auto-enrolment into a pension fund is not required. If the above criteria do not apply, you are breaking the law by neglecting to enrol your employees into a pension scheme. This will result in a fine, and potentially restriction of your right to do business.

How much you contribute to an employee's pension depends on their salary – and how much you're willing to pay. Essentially, a pension needs to total 8% of an employee's qualifying earnings. These earnings are complicated as there could be a number of factors at play, but for the sake of argument let's use an employee's gross pay.

This 8% contribution breaks down as:

- 3% paid by you, the employer – minimum.
- 4% paid by the employee.
- 1% paid by the government.

This means that, if you pay an employee £1,000 per month, you'll also need to pay an additional £30 into a pension pot each month. Your employee then pays £40 themselves (usually taken from their pay directly), and the government adds an additional £10, making £80 a month in total.

You can pay more if you're feeling generous. If you decide to pay £60, your employee only loses £10 of their pay. Remember, your contributions are tax-deductible.

Are you still with me? I appreciate that this was a very dry chapter. Sadly, it's all necessary information. Many small business owners run into trouble because the dull-but-essential obligations of tax and finance are not taken into consideration. Let's move onto altogether more wholesome topics – the nuts and bolts of running your business and taking care of dogs.

Chapter 5

Policies and Client Information

Before applying for your local authority licence or approaching potential clients, you'll need to work out your policies and procedures. You must have these in place before you start doing business. You will also need a customer contract. That's for your protection, and that of your clients – both canine and human.

When it comes to your customer contract, it's up to you as to whether you'd like to establish a time-bound contract. On the one hand, this will offer you a measure of protection. If you're working with clients on a good faith basis, they could pull the plug on your working relationship with no notice. This could leave you in a financial hole. By signing a client up to a commitment of three, six or twelve months at a time, you are – theoretically – guaranteeing income for that period of time.

There is a flipside to this, however. Contracts and loyalty work both ways. If you find that you're struggling to bond with a dog, the dog behaves inappropriately, or your human client rubs you the wrong way, you may be saddled with them until the end of the contract. You can enter 'unacceptable behaviour' break clauses into the contract that allow you to terminate early, but these need to be fair and reasonable.

To get started on your policies, make a list of key questions that will pertain to your business. You will need to build your policies around the answers to these. Examples of the questions that you should ask yourself include:

- How many dogs can you legally care for?
- What cross-section of dogs will you accept, in terms of sizes, ages, breeds, etc?
- Will you accept dogs that are not spayed or neutered? Up to what age?
- How will you manage problem behaviour from the dogs in your care?
- What constitutes unacceptable conduct, either from the dogs or their human owners?
- How will you approach walkies? Where will you take the dogs, how often, and for how long?
- Will you feed the dogs? If so, what quality of food is acceptable? How will you protect yourself against potential

allergic reactions that you were not warned about? Are the dogs allowed treats?
- Will you collect the dogs from their home and drop them off, or must the dogs come to you? A mix of both?
- What is a fair flat rate charge for your daycare service, and will you charge extra for additional services?
- How often will you invoice your clients – daily, weekly, monthly? Will you accept cash, cheque, bank transfer? Should you invest in a credit card machine? Money up front? Or something else?
- Should you request a deposit from clients to protect yourself against no-shows? Is the deposit fully refundable? How do you protect yourself – as fairly as possible – against last minute cancellations?
- Will you charge extra for late collections or drop-offs? Think about the impact this may have on your personal life.

You may be able to think of a number of additional questions to pose. Everybody's circumstances differ, and everybody has different priorities. Think carefully about what matters most to you and build your offering around this.

Questions for Your Clients

I will return to the discussion about policies for your business in a moment. First, let's talk about what you'll need to know about your potential lodgers.

Before agreeing to take a dog into your home, you need to gather as much information as you possibly can. You could be putting yourself, the dog or other canines at risk by bringing the wrong animal into your environment.

Your questions will centre on medical history, behaviour and routines.

Here are some sample questions to pull together at an exploratory meeting with a human client. You may wish to add some additional queries that are particularly relevant to you and your lifestyle.

What inoculations has your dog received and when?
A current veterinary vaccination record must be seen to ensure that dogs have current vaccinations against canine parvovirus, canine distemper, canine adenovirus/infectious canine hepatitis, leptospirosis and other relevant diseases.

Vaccination against other diseases such as kennel cough (Bordetella bronchiseptica / Canine parainfluenza virus) may be required by the establishment. Primary vaccination courses must be completed at least 2 weeks before boarding. Vaccines used must be licensed for use in the UK.

Are flea treatments up to date?
Do not accept no for an answer in this instance. A flea infestation can take hold quickly and be virtually impossible to fully dispose of. Fleas lay up to 50 eggs a day throughout their lifespan, and these eggs will lie dormant in your carpet and soft furnishings, waiting until they detect a warm host body before hatching. Unless you're keen on fumigating your house from top to bottom, and all the expense and upheaval that comes with that, do not entertain the notion of boarding dogs with fleas. Before you know it, you'll have an epidemic of parasites infecting all the dogs in your home. That will not go down well with owners, who will then experience the same frustrations in their own homes. Practice what you preach, too – remain updated on your own dog's treatments.

Is the dog spayed/neutered?
The reason for this question is obvious. If you don't want your home turning into a canine honeymoon suite, you're going to need a policy in place surrounding intact dogs. It's also worth knowing anyway, though. The behaviour of a dog changes after this surgery. It typically makes them much calmer and less territorial. A fixed-only policy is something that you may want to consider.
In-season bitches must not be accepted for boarding if intact males are on the premises. It's not a good idea in any circumstances but it will also contravene your licence if intact males are present.

How often does the dog usually walk, use the bathroom and eat?
Dogs are creatures of habit and routine. They have their little rituals in place, and they'll be considerably easier to care for if you stick to a pre-existing schedule. You may need to compromise, as multiple dogs will have multiple schedules, but you'll be able to come up with something if you're armed with enough information.

How is the dog praised, and how is their behaviour rectified?
You shouldn't really be bringing dogs into your home unless their owner has mastered training. Dog day care is not the same as dog discipline. You'll have your hands full, and you can't dedicate the attention required to rectifying unwanted behaviours. All the same, learn how the dog enjoys being praised – is it a stroke, a pat on the head, or a verbal cue? This will lead to more of the same, as canines love to please. Equally, learn any short, sharp verbal commands that may stop the dog getting themselves hurt. You don't want to punish them. That's not your dog, and it's usually

counter-productive anyway – dogs rarely understand punishments, and it only upsets them. If you can nip unwanted actions in the bud, you'll all get along better.

Is the dog vocal?

Barking can be a major problem when boarding dogs. As I have discussed previously, if you're not cautious your neighbours could report you as a nuisance due to barking. Find out what sparks barking behaviour (common examples include doorbells, being left alone and other dogs entering shared territory) and aim to avoid exposing dogs to these triggers.

Does the dog play well with others?

Obviously you can't consider housing a dog that doesn't get along with other pets, or children. Quiz the owner on how comfortable the dog is with strangers in different environments. Do not bring them into your home until you're certain that it's safe to do so.

What is the dog's favoured play style, and how playful are they?

I will discuss canine play styles in greater detail in our next chapter. Just be aware that different dogs like to play in different ways. You'll need to factor this into your day care offering. Pairing a large dog that loves wrestling with a small dog that is afraid of physical confrontation is no fun for anybody.

How does the dog behave on a walk? Do they have good recall?

You – or somebody that you employ – will need to take the dogs in your care for some exercise. That's the law. Before you do so, however, you'll need to know if it's safe to let the dog off their lead. Query, and test, the recall of the dog in question. If they respond to their own name, it's not an exaggeration to say that it may just save their life. For home boarded dogs, you need written consent from owners that permits walking with dogs from other households, and – where appropriate – to be allowed off-leash.

Does the dog have any allergies or medical concerns?

If the dogs in your care have any pre-existing medical issues, you *need* to know about this. It means you'll know exactly how to react in particular circumstances. I'll discuss managing ill health, allergies and personal injury in the next chapter.

Does the dog have any phobias or anxiety triggers?

Just like people, dogs can live with a range of worries and anxieties. Some dogs are carefree, and others are naturally neurotic. That doesn't necessarily need to be a problem, but you must be aware of it. If a dog is liable to freak out every time they see a bee, hear a vacuum or smell a cat, you'll need to assess whether your home is a safe space for them.

Is the dog prone to escape attempts?
Some dogs cannot resist the prospect of adventure. If they see an open door, they're going to bolt for it. It doesn't matter how happy they are in your home. If the dogs in your care are prone to this behaviour, you need to know about it. It goes without saying that you shouldn't leave doors open for prolonged periods anyway, but occasionally opening and closing doors is unavoidable. If you have a canine Houdini on your hands, ensure they're firmly behind closed doors or gates when the doorbell chimes.

Is the dog microchipped?
It is a legal requirement that a dog is microchipped. This will set your mind at rest a little if they *do* escape. At least a microchip will help them be reunited with their owner once captured. If the owner admits their dog is not microchipped, it's best not to do business with them. This suggests that their approach to pet parenting is cavalier at best (no spaniel-centric pun intended). If the dog is microchipped, consider having your details added to the central database as an emergency contact.

Who is the dog's emergency contact?
This is an obvious one. Sometimes, things happen. Important decisions may be necessary, or you could have to take the dog to a vet as a matter of urgency. If this is the case, you're going to need emergency contact numbers for the owners of the pooch. Ensure that you have a multitude of contact options so you can always get hold of somebody. If the owner is going on holiday, ensure they've not given you the details of their significant other. They will likely be on the same holiday. If not, you may have a poorly dog and a marital breakdown on your hands.

It's important to remember that *are* right and wrong answers to these questions. If your home is not suitable for the dog for any reason, do not take on the client. You'll end up doing more harm than good to your business, and the poor dog's psyche.

If you later find that a human client has not been entirely honest in answering these questions, it's best to part company. You could be opening yourself up to any number of future issues. Heartbreaking though it may be, some dogs require care above and beyond what you can provide. You need to consider the safety of your other canine clients.

Your Policies

As promised, let's take a closer look at some of the policies that you need to consider. Once you have thought about how you'll approach these matters, it's highly advisable to put them in writing. Contracts are not a legal requirement, but they may go a long way to protecting you.

The Dogs in Your Care

First and foremost, you need to think about the dogs that you're prepared to take into your home. Refer back to Chapter 3, where I discussed how many dogs you can take into your home legally. That's obviously your licence cap as to how many canine boarders that you can accept.

Just note what I've said here – that's the *maximum* number of dogs that you can take in. You're not legally obliged to fill your home to capacity. There are obvious advantages to doing so. More dogs equals more money, and more clients that could potentially spread the word about your business. It's also more expenses and more work, though. It's understandable if you would prefer a quieter life.

Next, you need to think about the dogs themselves. You obviously love dogs. You wouldn't be considering this line of work otherwise. Unfortunately, it's sad but true that not all dogs are created equal. That's why I devised the questions above. You need to know that bringing dogs into your home is not going to jeopardise the safety and quality of life of yourself, your family, your existing pets, other clients and your neighbours.

Refer back to the questions that I discussed and ensure that you're happy with the answers provided. Once you have covered those basics, you can start to dig a little deeper. There's plenty to consider before opening your doors to a new client.

- What is the breed of the dog? Does the temperament, size, play style and exercise needs of this dog tally up with your own availability, and the size and energy levels of the other dogs in your home? It's hardly fair to board a Shih Tzu with three Dobermans. No matter how good-natured the bigger dogs are, they will intimidate and dominate a toy breed.
- Is the dog used to sharing? Many dogs are doted upon by their owners. If the dog is being left with a professional carer all day, you can assume that he or she is well-loved. Casual or indifferent pet parents would not put their money where their mouth is. The downside to this is that the dog may be used to having things all their own way. Sharing blankets, food and toys may not sit well.

- Does the dog have behavioural issues? This is something that you need to be mindful of. A trial run with the dog before committing to a long-term working relationship is advisable. The truth is, an owner may see particular dog behaviours as quirky or charming. That's fine for them, but not for you. You need to be firm and clear about what is acceptable and what is not.

When it comes to matching dogs up, different breeds belong to different groups. There are seven types of dog. The breeds are broken down in the following table.

Dog Type	Example Breeds	Typical Persona
Herding	Border Collie, Sheepdog, Australian Cattle Dog.	Hugely energetic, playful, will chase *anything*, need a job to do.
Sporting	Golden Retriever, English/Irish Setter, Pointer, Brittany.	Energetic, high prey drive, excellent sense of smell, greedy.
Non-Sporting	Poodle, Dalmatian, French Bulldog.	Variable – this dog type has a very broad definition.
Worker	Husky, Mastiff, Akita, Boxer, Rottweiler, Doberman	Loyal, strong, energetic, intelligent, destructive if not stimulated.
Hound	Basset, Daschund, Greyhound, Beagle, Whippet.	Excellent sense of smell, greedy, quite lazy, affectionate.
Terrier	Yorkshire Terrier, Irish Terrier, Jack Russell.	Energetic, yappy, short-tempered with other dogs, high prey drive.
Toy	Pug, Shih Tzu, Bichon Frise, Pomeranian.	Affectionate, cuddly, non-sporty, low maintenance.

Some combinations could pose a challenge, so be wary of this. Dogs are flexible and considerably less judgmental than humans, though. Most of the time, different breeds and types can happily co-exist and become friendly. Maybe this will change if they ever invent a dog-friendly version of Twitter.

Food is another big consideration. First and foremost, you need to make a decision about whether you are going to feed the dogs in your care. If you do, it needs to apply to all. You can't offer a food bowl to three canines and leave another two to go hungry. They won't understand that orders have come from on-high. They'll just assume they're being ignored or punished, and quite possibly act out as a result.

If you are going to feed, however, there is a new range of questions that open up before you.

- What time will the dogs eat?
- Will they be fed kibble, wet food, raw or a combination?
- How much food is appropriate?
- Do any of the dogs have food aggression?
- Are the dogs allowed a post-dinner treat? Can they be treated throughout the day?

If you survey five dog owners with these questions, you'll likely receive five different sets of answers. That's why you'll need to have a strict policy in place and ensure that your human clients are completely familiar with it. This way, you can both make an informed decision as to whether the working relationship is destined to be a success.

It's best to make a list of every potential element of canine care and list out similar questions. That way you'll be ready for anything – though you'll no doubt still be taken by surprise on occasion. That's par for the course when working with dogs.

Unacceptable Canine Behaviour

The old adage goes that there is no such thing as a bad dog, just a bad owner. I happen to agree with that, but unfortunately it holds no relevance to this line of work. You're not lodging owners, you are lodging dogs. This means that you will need to draw a line in the sand, and have firm written policies in place surrounding what is considered inappropriate dog behaviour.

How you approach this is up to you. However, discuss how you will approach immediate behaviour correction with the dog's owner. Shouting at a dog doesn't help. It just gets them wound up. Physically reprimanding a dog is not just unhelpful, it's reprehensible. You need to discuss a technique that is mutually agreeable, such as a stern verbal command.

You'll also need to decide upon what is considered inappropriate behaviour in a dog. Basically, your endgame here is keeping everybody else in your home safe. It's not about running a household of impeccably behaved, silent, non-playful canines. That doesn't sound like any fun at all. There are certain no-nos for any day care business though, and your clients need to know this.

Suggested examples of unacceptable canine behaviour could include:

- Constant, unstinting barking.

- Aggression toward other dogs or people within the home.
- Aggression toward strangers (neighbours, postal delivery workers, etc.)
- Destructive behaviour.
- Regular attempts to escape the house
- Spot marking inside your home.

A dog may indulge in any or all of these actions to a small extent. *It's what dogs do*. If you're expecting none of the above, you're in for a rude awakening. Ultimately though, it's about deciding when enough is enough. If you don't feel safe in your home, or the expenses of managing bad behaviour outweigh the earnings of your business, it's time to part company.

There could be other reasons why you cease caring for a dog, too. These could include:

- **Incontinence, whether wilful or accidental**. If a dog has accidents in the home, it's never a good thing. You don't want to be cleaning up after them multiple times per day. It will also encourage other dogs to eliminate indoors in an act of solidarity.
- **Chronic anxiety**. If a dog is a bag of nerves around you and your home, it will only be a matter of time before the relationship goes south. A nervous dog will usually end up expressing their anxiety through aggression. Sometimes it's better to cut your losses in advance.
- **Unwillingness to exercise**. Some dogs will refuse to walk. They could be in pain, or they could just be lazy. Either way, you have a problem. You can't really leave the dog alone in your home, but the other dogs cannot miss out on their exercise either. Eventually, you'll need to make a decision. Under the terms of your licence, dogs in your home might not be allowed to be left unaccompanied or for no more than 3 hours maximum per day. Know your licensing obligations.

Finding yourself unable to look after a dog is often tragic. It's only natural that you'll want to do everything you can to help. Oftentimes, undesirable behaviour is a result of a poor start in life and cannot be overcome. Alas, you'll need to don your professional armour in these instances. Learn to apply boundaries and stick rigidly to them. The fact is, your business specialises in canine day care, not dog obedience training. You don't have the time, experience or knowhow to deal with these complex issues. The safety of yourself, the dogs of other clients and your family must always come first.

Having said all this, there is nothing to say that you cannot terminate a working relationship based on the actions of an owner. This is your business, and one of the privileges of being a business owner is choosing who you decide to work with.

If a dog's owner displays any of these behaviours, sever the relationship. Life is too short to put yourself through such problems.

- Aggressive or abusive behaviour.
- Consistent tardiness in collecting or dropping off dogs.
- Refusing to pay invoices, or chronic lateness in settling bills.

The moment you are getting less from a working relationship than you gain from it, it's time to move on. There are plenty of other clients in the world.

Collections and Drop-Offs

Having a policy about whether you'll collect dogs or not is more important than it may seem. You need to get a structure in place, including a timetable. You'll also need contingency plans for when things invariably go wrong through no fault of anybody.

Let's use a hypothetical example. You arrange for a dog to be dropped at your home by an owner at 7.30 am every weekday morning. This works for both parties. Your owner can drop the dog off on their way to work, and it leaves you time to get them settled before you tackle the school run.

Now, what happens if that client does not turn up until 8.15? Do you allow your children to be late for school, as you can't leave the house? Do you tell the client not to turn up at all, because they missed their slot? That hardly seems fair. The client could have been stuck in a traffic jam or faced any number of unexpected obstacles.

The same could also apply to picking up at the end of the working day, too. If you have a dog longer than expected, it could throw your entire evening into chaos. You may need to drop your children off at various clubs or activities. You may have an evening class to attend, or social plans. You may just want a few hours to yourself without being licked to death by a boisterous dog. Whatever the reason, a client turning up late to collect their dog can be troublesome.

Put a policy in place to determine how you will react to these scenarios. You'll have to be reasonable. A zero-tolerance response to any kind of tardiness is inadvisable – people won't feel happy working with you under such draconian rulings. However, it will benefit you to put some deterrents in place. Financial penalties for repeated offenses are usually effective, as long as they are fair and reasonable. In the meantime, ensure that the lines of communication are kept open and have a contingency plan where possible. A little flexibility goes a long way in maintaining a happy and harmonious working relationship.

Financial Matters

Last, but by no means least, I will address financial concerns. The cornerstone of your business, and something that you'll need to think about long and hard.

When it comes to weighing up financial policies, start with a list of questions that you'll ask yourself.

- How will you charge? By the hour, or by the day?
- How much will you charge for your services?
- What activities merit an additional charge on top of your standard rate?
- Will you issue any financial penalties on top of your existing charges?
- How often will you review your price plan?
- How often will you bill your clients?
- What forms of payment will you accept?
- What are your payment terms?
- For how long are your prices fixed?

This is plenty to think about. As is our custom, let's take a deeper dive into each of these questions.

What is a Fair Charge for Canine Daycare Services?

There are so many variables to this question that it’s impossible to answer for you.

- How much experience do you have?
- What qualifications do you have?
- Where in the UK are you based?
- How many competitors are your local area?
- Are you offering any additional services?

If you have competition, look at their pricing and react accordingly. It’s common practice to undercut the established businesses in town, but make sure that you’re realistic. Don’t forget the many and varied expenses that you’ll be occurring in you work. You need to pay for food, toys, beds, walking apparatus and who knows what else.

You also need to be careful about the reputation that you cultivate. Do you want a reputation for being the cheapest in town or the best? People's dogs are precious, and they expect a boarding/day care offering to reflect those values. A price that looks too good to be true will be met with suspicion. How could a skilled and competent person possibly offer their services so cheaply? You may be viewed as a dog-loving hobbyist that's looking to earn some pocket money and disregarded as a result. Of course, that's not even mentioning the fact that it's just a matter of time before somebody else comes along with the idea of undercutting you!

If you're offering a unique service, the world is your oyster. You can pick your pricing accordingly, based on what you consider fair. The part of the world you live in will obviously play a part in this. The cost of living in London and the surrounding areas will always be higher than, say, the Welsh Valleys.

First, sit down and write down all of the expenses that you expect to incur. That's all the dog-related peripherals that I just mentioned, plus all of your insurance policies. You'll need to ensure these are covered before you even think about charging for your time. If you're not earning enough to keep the dogs fed and entertained, you'll be out of business before you know it.

Next, factor in your experience and knowhow. Ultimately, people will be prepared to pay for expertise. That's why I recommend taking a range of courses before you start your business.

Finally, assess a fair and reasonable hourly rate for your time. Remember, the national living wage starts at £8.21 per hour so you really shouldn't be looking below £9. Add this hourly rate – based on your efforts and experience – to your anticipated expenses, and you have your answer.

What are Considered Fair Additional or Penalty Charges?

"Fair" is a subjective term. It's up to you if you would like to draw up a policy for additional charges. There may be times that you need to perform extra work outside the remit of your contract. You may consider this a favour, or you may want to charge for it.

Here's an example. You take the dogs out for a walk, as is standard, and one of them gets themselves utterly filthy and covered in mud. Dogs will do that – especially those with white fur. It's a universal truth.

In this instance, you'll want to bathe the dog when you get home. This will take time out of your day, and frankly, it may be a horrific experience. As I'll discuss in our next chapter, most dogs loathe and fear the bathtub.

Do you charge for this extra service? It would be fair to do so. It's not as though you are offering grooming services as part of your day care package. Equally however, a client may turn this back on you and say that it was your decision to take the dog to a muddy destination.

The same applies to damages to your home. If a dog chews a hole in your sofa, you will quite understandably want to charge for repairs. Likewise, if a dog destroys an ornament, you may want to be compensated. However, your clients may just say that you should have watched the dog appropriately and prevented such mishaps. Essentially, I am saying that you'll need to choose the hills that you're prepared to die on.

There are some matters that should *always* be written into your policy as additional charges, though. Veterinary bills, for example. If a dog is taken unexpectedly sick in your care, you'll rush them to the vet. You'll likely have to pay up-front for a consultation, and for any potential treatments. Even if the dog is insured by their owner, there will be an excess to cover. If this comes out of your pocket, be sure to write it into a contract that you expect to be reimbursed. You can then write this expense off on your tax return. Consider it compensation for your trouble and emotional turmoil.

How Often Should Clients to Billed?

When you're ready to bill your clients, draw them up an invoice. There are templates for this all over the internet, so it's nothing complicated. It just means that you have a formal record of what you are charging, and to who. This will become invaluable when balancing your books.

Next, decide how often you'd like to be paid. There are some key options here – always pre-paid, or weekly or monthly post-service? If you're providing very occasional services, you can draw up an ad hoc invoice.

Weekly payments will help your cash flow. You'll have a constant supply of money coming in, which will be helpful – you'll also have a constant flow of cash going *out* as you regularly replenish food supplies and the like. However, weekly invoicing also means more admin when you do your accounting.

Monthly invoicing is less work in the longer term. You just have to be mindful of your cash flow in the meantime. If some of your clients are slow to pay for whatever reason, will you have enough spare to cover the shortfall? Do not jeopardise repayments of your day-to-day expenses. If you can't meet your mortgage repayments, you'll have all kind of problems.

Choose which invoicing period works best for you, and progress accordingly. Write your billing frequency up as a policy, too. This way, no client can claim to be taken by surprise by an invoice.

What Payment Terms Should be Implemented?

There are two parts to this question. How will your clients pay you, and how long are you prepared to wait to be paid?

Firstly, assess how you'd like to be paid. There are pros and cons to every kind of transaction.

- Cash ensures immediate payment, but it can be tricky to keep track of. You'll need to maintain very strict financial records, including manual bookkeeping. It also leaves you vulnerable to accusations of financial mismanagement if audited.
- Direct bank transfers are very simple and ideal. It makes it easier to track your accounts, and your clients can set up a Direct Debit to avoid any late payments. This would be our advice for payment.
- Cheques are virtually obsolete. You'll be creating a rod for your own bank by accepting cheque payments. It's best to avoid these.
- If clients wish to pay online on an ad hoc basis, they can do so using Apple Pay or PayPal. This will be simple enough to arrange. Just be aware that you'll lose money in handling fees by using these services.
- You could invest in software that enables debit card payments too. You no longer need an old-fashioned, lumbering PDQ machine. Look into a service such as Square, iZettle, SumUp or Payzone to learn how you can do this.

Once you've established *how* you would like to be paid, you need to establish *when* you expect to be paid. The obvious answer is, "immediately upon issuing an invoice", but you'll need to have contingency plans.

What happens if a week or a month passes and you still have not received payment? Is it appropriate to continue offering the service when you have money outstanding? You don't want to punish the dog for the transgressions of their owner, but equally, you have a business to run. Speak to your human clients and find out what is happening. In addition, write a policy into your contract about late payment. Choose an acceptable cut-off time for your invoices and make it clear that withdrawal of services and/or fines will be issued beyond this point.

When is it Reasonable to Review Price Plans?

You'll see a theme emerging here …. that's up to you. However, I recommend being consistent with all clients.

Here is a suggested policy pertaining to cost reviews:

- All charges will be frozen for the first 12 months of working together.
- At the end of every financial year, you reserve the right to review your price plan.
- Any increase in cost will become active at the end of the existing contract (if applicable.)
- You will provide a minimum of 30 days of written notice for any price changes.

Base financial reviews of your costs upon your tax return. You may have noticed that you are spending more than anticipated on expenses, which is increasingly your outlay. Naturally, this means that you'll want to increase your prices to reflect this. Check the annual rate of inflation, too. You may wish to factor this into an annual price rise.

Chapter 6

The Nuts and Bolts of Canine Care

When that magical day arrives and you're ready to start welcoming dogs into your home, the real work begins.

I promised earlier in this book that I would give you an idea of what a day taking care of canine boarders will involve. I have to be honest – that was an empty promise. There is no hard and fast rule about what to expect from this business. Some days will be comparatively quiet, and others will be sheer chaos from start to finish. That's all part of the fun of working with dogs.

There are certain things that I would like to discuss, however. Particular matters that may fall under your jurisdiction. Throughout this chapter, we are going to discuss the following.

- How can you successfully manage walkies with multiple dogs?
- How should you play with the dogs in your care?
- What do you do if the dogs in your care will not stop barking?
- How should you react if two dogs in your care start fighting?
- How do you go about bathing the dogs in your care, if necessary?
- What happens if one of the dogs is taken ill under your care?
- How do you administer canine first aid in the event of injury or an emergency?

For your sake, and that of the dogs in your care, I'm hoping that some of this information will be irrelevant to you. I'd love nothing more than to hear that you never had to administer CPR to a dog, or that you never had to break up a fight when fur started to fly. All the same, wouldn't you agree that it's better to have this information and not need it, than find yourself in such a situation and having no idea about what to do?

Walking the Dogs

As I have previously discussed, walking the dogs in your care is a legal requirement. You need to take them out for a minimum of 20 minutes of exercise, subject to breed, age, health and weather conditions. Realistically, however, you should be looking at something better than this. An hour is ideal. That also gives you the opportunity to take a break, stretch your legs and get some exercise yourself. One of the best things about working with dogs for a living is the ability to stay fit without needing to join a gym.

Before you tackle this, however, ask yourself a handful of questions.

- Are you physically fit and strong enough to walk the dogs yourself? Are you nimble and fleet of foot enough to chase after a canine that makes a break for it? If not, you may need to look into hiring a dog walker to assist you.
- How will you group the dogs? Are you taking all the dogs in your care out at the same time? If that's the case, you need to ensure that they're compatible in terms of size and energy. If not, you'll have to take them out separately – which throws up a new list of logistical questions.
- Where will you take the dogs? Off-lead time is ideal if you can trust the canines in question to return when called. This suggests that you'll need to take them somewhere with plenty of open space – but in doing so, you also need to factor in a new range of behavioural questions.
- How will you walk the dogs? There's more to dog walking than just taking a long stroll and shouting. "heel!" every once in a while. You'll need eyes in the back of your head and a constant state of cat-like awareness.

With all of this in mind, let's take a deeper look into the art of exercising dogs.

Grouping Dogs

Before you even entertain the idea of taking your dogs out, find out how many dogs you can legally be in charge of at any given time. Your local council may have strong views on this, in fact they may have specific bylaws and violating their doctrines could leave you facing a fine. If there are no regulations, six is the maximum for home boarded dogs under the terms of your licence, assuming no local authority caps, and that any dog walker can realistically handle. Even then, you may be pushing your luck a little. The RSPCA and the Dogs Trust specify 4 is the maximum.

It may make your life easier to invest in a splitter lead. This way, you can attach one lead to all the dog's harnesses (always use a harness when walking multiple dogs, never a collar), rather than attempting to carry multiple leads.

You'll also need to group the dogs according to their breed, size, energy levels, age, health and general behaviour. Not all dogs are the same, and a dog walk can quickly turn into a living nightmare if you do not plan properly. For example, if you try to walk a Border Collie, a Pug and a Daschund at the same time, you'll be in a world of trouble.

- The Collie will be champing at the bit to get off-lead and chase anything that moves. If you encounter any wildlife, heaven help all of you. The Collie will pull the entire time, desperate to reach the eventual destination.
- The Pug will be alert and mischievous, and likely desperate to keep pace with the Collie. Unfortunately, a Pug's little legs find it impossible to match a bigger dog stride for stride. The Pug will soon be out of breath – and for a brachycephalic breed, that's hugely dangerous.
- As for the Daschund? Well, they might be completely disinterested in all of these shenanigans. This sometimes-lazy breed will be just as passionate about staying at home and napping on the sofa as the Collie will be about getting out. You'll be forcefully pulled into two different directions.

This is why it's so important to think about different breeds when you take on your clients. Always factor the exercise needs of different dogs into your thinking. Some need a physical workout, others prefer mental exercise routines. This doesn't mean that you can't have a variety of breeds under your remit, but you won't necessarily be able to deal with them all yourself. You'll need additional help and support.

You have a handful of options when it comes to bringing in a third party to help you out.

- All walk together, with your assistant handling all the larger or smaller dogs. Your assistant can pick up or drop pace where necessary. This is not advised. Remember, dogs are pack animals – and humans are part of the pack. The dogs will grow confused, and potentially upset, if walking at different rates with different handlers. Plus, it's quite intimidating for other members of the public when faced with 4-6-8 or 12 dogs, all off the lead hairing towards them, and that assumes they'll respond to your immediate voice commands.
- Your assistant takes the larger or smaller dogs on a different walk – longer for the large, energetic breeds, shorter for the smaller, lazier dogs.
- You take the dogs out in shifts, with your assistant staying home with those that are not being walked. This means plenty of exercise for you, but less time at home taking care of your business – and more hours payable to an employee.

It's really up to you how you handle this conundrum. It's important that you come to an arrangement that suits the dogs as much as you, though. Walkies should be among the highlight of many dog's days. A stroll with their friends even more so. Matching dogs up with incompatible walking partners, and having to cut short their exercise because of it, is not fair on your canine clients.

To Muzzle or Not to Muzzle?

Muzzling dogs is a controversial subject, and an often misunderstood one. Let's be clear, a dog with a muzzle – especially a larger breed – can be a scary sight. You wouldn't be blamed for crossing the street to avoid engaging with such a beast. They look like some kind of canine Hannibal Lecter.

The fact is though, not all dogs are muzzled due to antisocial behaviour. While it's true that muzzles are primarily associated with preventing barking and biting, dogs also explore the world with their mouths. This can become problematic when they decide to eat everything they come into contact with.

Some dogs take bizarre pleasure from eating stones and pebbles. Broken teeth and digestive issues will follow. Some dogs cannot resist lapping water from puddles. These will be packed with bacteria and fungi, potentially leading to serious illness. Some dogs will gleefully snaffle plants, berries and mushrooms – any number of which could be toxic, and lead to a major health emergency.

Of course, there are downsides to muzzles. The aesthetics, and the potential for reduced fun, is only part of the story. On a hot day, a dog on a lengthy walk risks dehydration. A muzzle will restrict the ability to drink from an appropriate water source. A tight muzzle may even prevent cooling off through panting. Brachycephalic breeds will also need a specialist muzzle, which resembles a gas mask.

Speak to a dog owner about how their pet behaves on a walk and decide whether a muzzle may be necessary. If you're going to muzzle one dog, it may be advisable to consider muzzling all. Dogs pick up on these differences, and you don't want one pooch to feel like they are being punished. This will make them reluctant to come and stay with you in the future.

Where to Take the Dogs

The next question on your list is where you should take the dogs for their exercise. Do you simply walk them around the local shopping centre for an hour and let them take in some people watching, or do you for some serious off-lead time?

Factors to weigh up when deciding where to take the dogs include:

- Do the dogs have good recall?

- Do the dogs understand that other animals are not to be chased?
- Do the dogs tend to bark at other dogs or strange humans?
- Do any of the dogs have phobias or fears?
- Do you have access to a vehicle to transport the dogs for long distances?
- If so, are the dogs happy to enter a vehicle?
- Do you know the lay of the land, if one of the dogs runs off?
- Are all the dogs microchipped if the worst happens?

As you'll see, there is a lot of think about. This is important, though. It's tempting to just say that dogs should be allowed to be dogs and run free, and that's a noble bit of blue sky thinking. What happens when a dog starts chasing sheep, though? Section 9 of the Animals Act of 1971 states that a farmer can legally shoot a dog if they, "believe it is the only reasonable way of stopping [the dog from] worrying livestock." Is that a conversation that you want to have with a dog's owner?

Equally, you need to know if a dog is liable to be spooked by anything. Based on personal experience, dogs can be frightened by all manner of seemingly innocuous things. Motorcycle helmets, crutches and wheelchairs, skateboards and high-vis jackets are just some of the things that set off a dog, especially if they were previous mistreated. Likewise, some dogs are afraid of men with beards or black Labradors. All of these things must be taken into consideration before choosing where to walk the dogs in your care. You need to be mindful of what you're exposing them to.

Finally, no matter where you are, remember one thing. Always carry a substantial amount of poo bags and clean up after the dogs in your care! Not only is failing to do so antisocial and unpleasant, but it's a criminal offense. If spotted, you could face an on-the-spot fine of £80.

Entertaining Dogs on a Walk

Finally, you have to think about how you're going to entertain the dogs in your care. Some breeds will be happy just to walk, and to run in circles. For others, walking gets dull. They expect to be played with, or otherwise provided with stimulation.

If you're lucky, the dogs will play together. This will make your post-walkies life considerably easier. If the dogs chase each other, or play hide and seek, they'll be physically and mentally exhausted afterward. This means that you'll likely have a pack of napping dogs in your hands by the time you get home. That will free up an afternoon to catch up on your paperwork and tackle some other administrative tasks.

For this to happen, however, the dogs need to have compatible play styles. Larger dogs love to charge and knock each other off their feet, for example. If both dogs enjoy this game, it's fine. They'll take it in turns to be knocked into. If a big dog attempts it on a smaller counterpart, however, it will scare the life out of the poor little critter. Rough play is not for everybody.

Different dogs also enjoy different activities. Some canines love to swim and will hurl themselves into the nearest river during the summer months. Others are borderline phobic of water but live to play fetch. A walk without a tennis ball is no walk at all for those dogs.

You need to keep all the dogs amused so they'll enjoy their walk – but you can't take your attention off any one of them in favour of focussing on another. While one dog is swimming, another may be disturbing a nest of wasps nearby. Keep a close eye on every dog in your care.

Coping with Barking Dogs

Barking dogs can drive you – and everybody around you – barking mad. Barking is one of the most important behaviours to get under control in your business. As soon as one dog starts, it will usually set off the rest. Before you know it, you'll have an unappealing canine choir on your hands.

Some of the most common reasons for a dog to bark include:

- **Gaining Your Attention**. Dogs bark to get your attention. This could be to inform you that there is an intruder on your property. The postman is the arch nemesis of many dogs, after all. Alternatively, the dog may be informing you that they are hungry, thirsty, too hot, too cold, need use of the bathroom, are feeling ignored and neglected ... the list of potential explanations is endless.
- **Separation Anxiety**. Many dogs are distressed at the idea of being parted from their owners. This could manifest as distressed barking. Your dog will stand and bark at the door, hoping their owner will return to collect them.
- **Excitement**. Sometimes, a dog simply barks as an exclamation of glee and excitement. The dog is thrilled at the idea of being taken out, seeing a friend, or the smell of food. Barking is how they express this happiness. Just don't let it go too far.
- **Nature**. Some breeds of dog are genetically pre-disposed to bark. Terriers, for example, are hugely vocal. In these cases,

all you can do is manage the habit the best you can. Distractions are a great arsenal in your toolbox.

Barking for attention is something that you need to work on. If the dogs in your care realise that barking gets a response, they won't think twice about turning it to their advantage. You'll be barked at whenever a dog wants food, attention, playtime, walkies or just about anything else.

Do not use corrective behaviours on a barking dog. Punishment will just aggravate the scenario – and the owner of the pet will likely be displeased. Shouting at the dog to stop will just make them bark all the louder – the animal just thinks that you're joining in with the animated conversation. 'Shock collars', which give the dog a minor electric shock, are not just cruel but they're also ineffective. They will react to any sound, so a dog will be shocked whenever another animal barks.

If you are at your wits end, you may wish to consider a muzzle. You'll need a specialist muzzle here, different to what you'd use when taking the dog for a stroll. Discuss your options with a pet shop sales assistant. You'll need something soft that still enables the dog to eat and drink. The idea of a muzzle is to leave the animal exhausted if they try to bark to excess.

It's better to learn why the dog is barking and train them out of the habit, however. Ask the owner if the dog is vocal at home. This way, you can learn it's a personality trait or related to being placed in day care. From here, you can take the appropriate action.

Managing Separation Anxiety

Separation anxiety can be a major issue with dogs. Don't take it personally if a dog cries, howls and barks when their owner departs. This barking is an attempt at alerting their owner that they've been abandoned or kidnapped, and that they need to be rescued. Hopefully, they'll settle down eventually. All the same, you need to get them calm and keep the barking under control – think of the neighbours. Establish a new, calming routine as early as possible.

To manage separation anxiety, we must *understand* separation anxiety. Dogs freak out at the prospect of being separated from their owners for a number of reasons.

- Dogs consider their human families as part of their pack, and their owners as the alpha. The dog fears they are being banished from the pack.
- Dogs have no real concept of time – they live exclusively in the moment. They're not thinking ahead to eight to ten hours

in the future when they'll be reunited. They're worried about the here and now.

- Dogs cannot look after themselves. Paws lack opposable thumbs, after all. When an owner leaves a dog behind, the dog sees the person they trust to meet their needs walking away.

You're unlikely to ever *cure* separation anxiety. Some breeds are particularly prone to it, as are certain rescue dogs with trauma in their past. All you can do is manage the neurosis as best you can. To an extent, exposure will help with this. Dogs love routine, and eventually being left with you will become part of their daily expectation. Use that time to build a bond of trust.

In the meantime, you may need to investigate calming techniques. These could include:

- Aromatherapy.
- Distracting with play.
- Music.
- Massage.
- Thundershirts (check your local pet shop for these garments. Designed for thunderstorms, these vests compress a dog's pressure points and keep them calm.)

You'll also need help from the dog's owner. Make sure they do not make a fuss when they leave. If the owner spends five minutes showering a dog with cuddles, kisses and apologies for leaving, the dog will understandably wonder if they're ever coming back. Have the owner slip out while the dog is distracted. If they can be dropped off when other canines are already in situ, so much the better. Dogs are always much happier leaving one pack behind if they can immediately spend time with another.

Creating a Comfortable Environment

If a dog feels uncomfortable, they'll bark. They're trying to alert you to something. The ideal dog environment involves:

- Space to run and jump.
- Some form of mental stimulation.
- Company, whether human or canine in nature.
- Lack of sudden loud noises. If you live close to a source of noise, consider buying a white noise machine to neutralise the sounds for your houseguests.
- Body temperature of 38-39°C.
- Access to fresh, clean water.
- Easy access to an outside area.

Deprive the dogs in your care of any of these things, and you can expect them to voice their displeasure in no uncertain terms.

Calming Down a Barking Dog

No matter how much time you dedicate to preventing a dog from barking, you can't fight animal instinct. Dogs will bark, just as sure as night follows day. Sometimes, all you can do is react after the event.

First, try turning your back on the dog. If they are barking for attention, turning your back on them will quickly show that this is ineffective. As soon as the dog calms down, make a fuss of them. Show them that staying calm gets results much faster than shouting. You can even try walking out of the room. Just be aware that, if the dog is prone to separation anxiety, this will likely aggravate the issue.

If this doesn't work, check your surroundings for something that may be exciting for the dog. Close any windows and curtains – there may be people coming and going outside. You may also need further distraction techniques. Try tuning your radio to Classic FM. Classical music is believed to be calming for canines, and this will draw their attention away from other noises. If you live near a school, building site or other noisy property, this is particularly advisable.

As a last resort, calm the dog down with one-on-one attention. Offer soothing petting and strokes, gently reassuring the dog that everything is fine. I call this a last resort because you will potentially set a dangerous precedent. The dog may associate barking with attention in future. All the same, it's better than falling out with your neighbours.

Playing with Dogs

The best thing about working with dogs is that it takes them a long time to grow out of playtime. Dogs don't just *like* to play – they *need* to. It keeps their minds stimulated and provides exercise. Perhaps most importantly, it strengthens the bond between a dog and a human. You want your canine clients to actively enjoy coming to stay with you, surely?

Playing with dogs takes many forms, so you'll need to know what kind of games the dogs in your care enjoy. Popular dog games include:

- **Chasing**. Most dogs simply adore chasing each other. If things are going well, they'll take it in turns to the chaser and chasee.

- **Fetch**. Throw a ball or a frisbee and every dog in a mile-wide radius will chase it. This classic game is all linked to a dog's prey drive. Many canines are instinctively programmed to give chase when something moves at speed.
- **Wrestling**. Many larger dogs enjoy the rough-and-tumble of playfighting and wrestling. As long as this stays as play and doesn't devolve into a fight, and both dogs are on-board, it's fine.
- **Body Slamming**. Some dogs think it's hilarious to run up to another and try to knock them off their feet. Again, if both dogs are into this it's nothing to worry about.
- **Tug of War**. Dogs love to test their strength. If there's a sturdy stick or piece of rope on the ground, don't be surprised if a pair of canines take an end each and tug away.

Here's another way to look at it. Remember our table back in Chapter 5, where we discussed the different kinds of dogs and their temperaments? Let's revisit it, but now we're talking preferred playstyles.

Dog Type	Favoured Games
Herding	However you play with a herding dog, you need to keep them active. These dogs have energy to burn. They must also be intellectually stimulated. Fetch is a favourite, and they also enjoy chasing games. Just ensure they do not nip the heels of other dogs.
Sporting	Sporting dogs are all about the physicality. They like running and chasing, body slamming, wrestling and fetching. Many sporting dogs also enjoy water games.
Non-Sporting	As with describing personalities, this dog type is so broad that a particular play style cannot be assigned to them. Get to know the dog in question and learn their play style through trial and error.
Worker	Worker dogs are physical and enjoy wrestling, body slamming and play fighting. They can be quite serious and sometimes underestimate their own strength. Working dogs are best left to play with each other. They could accidentally hurt smaller dogs.
Hound	Hounds love to hunt. Nosehounds, such as Bassets, Daschunds and Beagles, follow scents. Sighthounds, such as Greyhounds and Whippets, will chase anything small they notice.
Terrier	Chasing, body slamming and wrestling. Terriers like to play rough. Be mindful of these dogs. They rarely play well with others and may start fights with dogs outside of their type. It will be like living with Scrappy Doo.
Toy	Toy dogs are all about the attention. They'll play soft and gentle games with each other, perhaps batting a ball around with their paws. Ideally though, they prefer a cuddle from a human.

The above is just a rough guide, largely based on stereotypes. Every dog is different, so the pets in your care may contradict this information. It's a good starting point though, and a great way to test playtime with the dogs in your care. Work out what kind of play works for them, and tailor their recreation time accordingly. It will be in your best interest to do so. The more you tucker dogs out with play, the sleepier and lower maintenance they'll be throughout the rest of the day.

You don't necessarily need to separate larger and smaller dogs in play. Small dogs often have big hearts and want to play with their larger friends. This will build their confidence. Likewise, playing with smaller dogs may teach bigger dogs to be gentle and considerate of their size. Just avoid skewing the ratio too much. One small dog among a pack of larger animals will end badly – the little pooch will end up getting hurt in the process. Likewise, one large dog amidst a swath of small breeds will feel like the lone adult at the children's table.

How to Tell if a Dog Wants to Play

Dogs can't speak to tell us what they want, so they rely on certain physical and verbal cues. The two most common examples of this are barking, and simply sitting down and staring into our eyes. You'll need to work out for yourself what your dog wants, most of the time.

Play is an exception to this. Dogs indulge in what is known as the, "play bow", in which they drop their head and wag their tail. This is the dog inviting you – or another canine – to instigate play. What you'll need to be mindful of is ensuring that dogs want to *continue* to play. Watch the dogs in your care. Play should always be a two-way street.

The two animals should take it in turns to be dominant and submissive. If one dog seems to be doing all the chasing, or all the wrestling, it could be less play and more bullying. If one dog tries to walk away and another keeps blocking them off or dragging them back, this is another warning sign. Be mindful of when play turns bad.

Dealing with Dog Fights

Dealing with fighting dogs is one of the most frightening experiences you'll have. If you're lucky, it will never happen. Dogs rarely resort to physical confrontation and will always give each other plenty of opportunities to back out first. Most of the time, they want to be left alone. If the time comes to deal with a dog fight, however, you'll need to follow a particular protocol.

- Separate the dogs (not directly at the head end!)
- Check yourself for any injury.
- Check the dogs for signs of injury.
- Apply first aid where necessary.
- Attempt to re-introduce the dogs once both have cooled off.

You must inform the owners of both dogs about what happened. In most cases, as long as both animals are unharmed and have made friends again, there will be nothing more to say. Be prepared for a client to look into removing their dog from your care though, especially if their pet was not the instigator of the conflict. It may seem unfair, but it's understandable. Factor this into your policies when drawing up contracts for your clients.

Why Would Dogs Fight?

Even the friendliest of dogs can sometimes find themselves in confrontation. This is especially likely if the dogs are not used to sharing spaces or resources. If a dog lives alone at home, they may find it overwhelming to share a space with other animals.

The most common battles that dogs will fight are related to:

- Jealousy over attention.
- Food aggression.
- Overstimulation.
- Annoying, excessive attention and requests to play.
- Disputes over territory or a favourite toy.
- Rough play gone bad.
- Excessive testosterone from two unfixed males.

Note that there is a big difference between a quick snap and a growl, and a fight. The former is very common, especially from older dogs to younger. It's how the younger dog learns manners. When they reach and breach the patience of an older dog, they are put in their place. Nobody has fallen out, and everybody is safe. A fight is when teeth are bared and claws are unsheathed. The term, "fighting tooth and nail" exists for a reason. Thankfully, genuine scrapping is rare.

Learn the Warning Signs of a Dog Fight

Dogs rarely go from 0 to 60. If two dogs are going to fight, they will typically give all manner of warnings to each other. These are also warnings for *you*. It means you'll have plenty of time to separate the warring canines before things get physical, assuming you react in time.

Signs to look out for include:

- Dogs circling each other.
- Dogs growling at each other.
- Dogs intensely barking at each other,
- Dogs making themselves look big.
- Dogs frantically wagging their stiff, rigid tails.

This is the canine equivalent of two schoolchildren in the playground shouting, "yeah? Come on then!" over and over. The dogs are each hoping that the other will walk away. Unfortunately, doggy ego can be a dangerous thing. It's possible that neither dog will want to be the one to back down. In such an instance, physical conflict becomes increasingly likely.

You may find that a third dog also starts barking and snarling. This dog is unlikely to want to get involved in the fight. Quite the opposite – this dog is attempting to defuse the situation. Think of this behaviour as the canine equivalent of the sobbing woman outside the local pub screaming, "leave him Gary, he's not worth it!"

Breaking Up a Fight

If you see two dogs fighting, you need to break them up ASAP. When a dog has their blood up, they can become increasingly vicious and determined to finish a fight. You also need to take care of yourself during this process, though. Don't wade in blindly, waving your arms and shouting. This will just aggravate the dogs further. They'll continue to hurt each other, and potentially turn their attention on you.

To break up a dog fight:

- Distract the dogs with a short, sharp noise, like a whistle or an air horn. This may be enough to break the spell.
- Get something between the dogs ASAP. Do not put any part of your body near their mouths – they'll mistake this for aggression and bite. Your intention is to break the eye contact between the animals. Use piece of paper or card if you can.
- Lead the dogs away in separate directions. You could really do with a second pair of hands to help with this. Two people means you can each care for an individual dog.
- Lock the dogs in different rooms. Stay with them during this time out. Make a fuss too, if they allow you to. This is not a punishment. You are giving the dogs a chance to cool off.

You will need to check yourself for any sign of injury. If you were bitten or scratched in breaking up the fight, deal with that before anything else. Once you're confident that you are fine, check the dogs for injuries. Look for bleeding, and if you find any wounds, tend to them ASAP.

Remember how I explained back in Chapter 3 that a canine first aid certificate is mandatory in my mind? This is one of the reasons why. You *must* be able to respond accordingly if something happens to the dogs in your care. However, to be on the safe side, I will cover a refresher on canine first aid later in this chapter.

Dealing with a Dog Bite

If you have been bitten by a dog, you need to take care of yourself. Don't just write it off as one of those things. You risk swelling, inflammation and infection if you don't take appropriate measures.

Check yourself for any injuries as soon as the dogs are separated. You'll be tempted to check the dogs first. Treat this experience like being on a plane, though. During air travel, you're advised to put on your own air mask first during an emergency, then help others. The same applies here. You'll be much calmer and more efficient if you know you're not injured.

If the dog bite did not break the skin:

- Run the bitten area under a cold tap for a few minutes. Wash it with unscented soap.
- Dry yourself off.
- Dab some kind of antibiotic oil over the bitten area. You're unlikely to suffer infection but better safe than sorry.
- Put a plaster over the bitten area to keep it clean and dry.

If the dog bite broke or punctured the skin:

- Wash the wound in cold water until the water runs clear.
- Once clean, elevate the wound to stem the bleeding.
- Dry the wound and wrap a bandage around it.
- Apply an antibiotic ointment to the wound.

If it's been ten years since your last tetanus shot, see your GP to rectify this. You must also keep an eye on the bitten area in the coming days. If it starts to swell, speak to your doctor. Dog mouths are breeding grounds for bacteria. If you have an infection, it needs to be treated with antibiotics. While that’s unlikely if the bite didn’t break the skin, it’s far more possible if you’re bleeding.

You are also required to inform the owner of the dog that you were bitten. You may decide that is unacceptable behaviour, and that you do not wish to board that dog any longer. That's entirely your decision, and it's one that nobody will judge you for. You also need to decide whether to take things further.

By this, I mean reporting the dog to the police. If that's a road you decide to go down, be aware of the consequences. There is every chance that the dog will be considered dangerous, and the owner will be forced to destroy the animal. The owner could also be facing a six-month prison sentence, fine of up to £5,000 and a lifetime ban from keeping another pet.

This all sounds draconian and it's presumably something you'll be keen to avoid. If the bite was an accident, and out of character for the dog, that's fine. Just be sure to inform the owner about what happened. If the dog bites somebody else, they may not be as understanding as you.

The Aftermath

One thing that you will likely notice is that both dogs are rather sheepish after a fight. They may even be a little traumatised. The fact is, most dogs hate fighting. It's not in their nature at all. Shock will start to set it as they realise what just happened.

Keep the dogs separated for a while and keep them calm. Pet them, talk to them, soothe them, and let them know that they're not in any trouble. You may not be impressed with the behaviour of an aggressive dog, but this is not the time for discipline. Explain what happened later to the owner – but ensure that they do not take action either. The dog will have long moved on from this incident by then and will not connect any punishment to the fight.

Once both dogs are calm again, let them out of their time out. Keep both dogs on their respective leashes and let them approach each other. This will be the start of the apology ritual. If there is any sign of renewed hostility, pull the dogs away and separate them again. What's more likely is that they'll sniff each other's faces. This will then lead to the patented sniff of each other's bottoms. By this point, the dogs have formally apologised.

Do be mindful of any future disagreements between these dogs. Canines do not hold a grudge, but they can develop a serious fear. If one dog is afraid of the other, they cannot really lodge together any further. You'll have to make a decision about which client to part company with. It's simply unfair to allow a dog to continually enter an environment that makes them anxious and nervous.

Giving a Dog a Bath

A dog that enjoys being bathed is a rare dog indeed, Unfortunately, it may be unavoidable on occasion.

I do not recommend offering bathing as a default part of your offering. Hygiene is the responsibility of a pet parent. You may take a dog for a walk and it comes home caked in mud however, or worse. If a dog gets a whiff of something interesting, they'll roll around in it. Sadly, the poop and pee of other animals – most notably foxes – is like perfume to domesticated canines.

The best ways to counter this? A blend of tomato ketchup, white vinegar and Animology's Fox Poo shampoo. You'll find the latter in any major pet shop.

In these situations, bathing is really the only option. Failing to do means you'll have a filthy house and a client that is most displeased to be handed a mucky pup at the end of their working day. Buckle up, though. The dog is unlikely to make this easy for you.

Why Do Dogs Hate Baths?

Nobody is quite sure why dogs are so bath averse. Many canines will gleefully swim in a river, so it's not always water related. Possible reasons for dogs to kick up a stink at the prospect of being bathed include:

- The shampoo you're using smells strongly or hurts their skin. You must *never* use human shampoo on a dog. They have very different skin pH to us.
- The water is too hot. Dogs like lukewarm water.
- You're spraying water straight in their face. Most dogs hate this.
- The bath is too small and the dog feels trapped.

The reason why dogs hate bathing isn't really yours to understand. What matters most is how you're going to get them clean where necessary.

Getting a Dog into the Bath

Never, ever force a dog into the bath. Wrestling with them only makes things worse. You'll end up with a dog that's scared of you. At best, the dog won't want to stay at your house any longer and you'll be down a client. At worst, you'll be bitten. Getting a dog into the bath is all about the carrot, not the stick.

- Put some toys in the bath.
- Smear the sides of the bath with peanut butter, or another favoured lickable treat.

- Pop something on the floor of the bath so it's less slippery. No dog likes to feel like Bambi on ice.

Convincing a dog to get into the bath may be a two-person job. If you simply cannot do it, think about reinforcements. It may advisable to have a mobile dog groomer on speed dial that will respond to short notice requests.

The Act of Bathing a Dog

OK, so you have the dog in the tub and you're good to go. You're now at a very delicate stage of the process. The dog can – and will – attempt to escape at a moment's notice. Here's what to do.

- Get everything you need in one place, within your arm's reach. That means towels, flannels, shampoo and a stiff drink for when you're done.
- Close the bathroom door. The dog *will* try to escape. If they do so, you'll have a combination of mud, soap suds and wet paw prints all over your home.
- Start running lukewarm water. Let the dog splash around in it. That may make the whole bathing experience less intimidating.
- Do whatever you can to keep the dog calm. Some canines react well to classical music, and lavender or frankincense scents is commonly referred to as canine relaxants. Rescue Remedy is also pet-safe, but the dog's owner may not take kindly to the use of human medications.
- Work methodically. Don't be tempted to rush the shower to get it over with quickly – you'll just panic the dog. Work slowly but steadily, leaving the face and head until last.

A good point is worth repeating here – *you cannot use human shampoo on dogs*. These products are designed to appeal to human senses. As well as the skin imbalance, they're loaded with scented chemicals. You'll inflict a lot of pain, and potentially an allergic reaction, on a dog using human shampoo.

If the dog is aggressive, you'll need to take some additional precautions. Gloves are advisable, and you may even want to consider a muzzle. Remember that the dog will be in a foul mood by the time you're done, especially if you muzzle them.

Drying the Dog Off

Many dogs enjoy air drying – after a good shake. When a dog shakes, they remove up to 70% of the water soaked into their fur. You'll end up drenched when they do it, but that's what you get for putting them through the bath time experience.

If it's a sunny day outside, give the dog a thorough rubdown with a soft, fluffy towel and let them outside. Five minutes in the sun will leave the canine as dry as a bone, if you'll forgive the turn of phrase. Just try to make sure they don't get filthy all over again.

If necessary, you could turn a hairdryer on the dog. Test how they react first. Hairdryers are noisy and can be scary. If the dog lets you use such an appliance, turn the heat down low and keep the dryer at a safe distance. Some dogs love this and treat it like they're at a spa. Others will be nervous, quivering wrecks. If the dog in your care falls under the latter category, stop using the hairdryer and leave them to air dry.

If you find yourself regularly needing to bathe and dry dogs, book an appointment with a groomer and seek some advice on the best products to use. You could even buy a dog-specific hairdryer that operates at a lower heat than a human equivalent.

Notify the owner of the dog if you needed to bathe them and show them what products you used. Dog skin and fur can be damaged if bathed too frequently, so the owner will want to avoid giving the dog a bath themselves for a few days. In addition, they'll need to know what products you used in case the dog has a delayed allergic reaction.

Cleaning a Dog Without a Bath

If bathing and showering a dog is out of the question, you can fall back on a couple of options. They may make the dog bearable to be around for the rest of the day. You can then hand them over to an owner to finish the job once your shift is over. If you do this, however, prepare for a backlash. A dog owner has left their pet with you to care for them. Returning them filthy and smelly because you let them romp around in a muddy field is not going to endear you to anybody.

If you're prepared to take that chance, use any of the following:

- Wet wipes.
- Dry shampoo. Test a tiny patch of fur first to ensure your dog's skin will not react poorly to this.
- Brush the dog with a fine-toothed comb.

Any of these will do a very temporary job. They're no substitute for a real wash, though. A Hozelock 7L portashower or Mud Daddy 8L portable shower could also help.

Taking Care of a Sick or Injured Dog

It's always possible that a dog will become unwell or be injured while in your care. This can be a worrying situation, as unless you're a trained vet you'll likely be unsure as to how to proceed.

I need to get something clear from the off. I'm not a vet and I don't want to give the idea that I'm impersonating one in this book. However, experience gives us some idea of how to care for a sick or injured dog. You'll feel much more confident confronting a concern if you can recognise it. This is one of the many reasons why I insist that you take a first aid course before looking after dogs.

It's best to have a policy in place for handling a dog that is taken unwell or hurt in your care. At the first sign of a problem, do you call the dog's owner and request that the canine is picked up to avoid the spread of a contagious disease or panic? Or do you rush them straight to the vet, ensuring that you have an update and professional opinion to share with said owner?

If the latter, do you have a contingency plan for who will look after other dogs in your care while you look after this one? No canine enjoys a trip to the vet. Taking a whole bunch of them, most of whom will not require treatment, is a recipe for chaos. Naturally, however, this may not be optional in the cases of severe injury. You *cannot* leave a dog to suffer because it's inconvenient to get to a vet.

Obviously, you'll also need to have a policy about whether you'll accept a dog that's under the weather into your home. Dogs, just like humans, can be prone to coughs, colds and sniffles. These can spread like wildfire amongst the canine population.

In most cases, *you'll* be safe. Cold and 'flu viruses are species-specific, and those that impact on dogs will not infect a human. Fungal infections (such as ringworm) and stomach bugs are exceptions to this rule, though. Tread very carefully if you have reason to believe that a dog is carrying one of these conditions.

Let's run the rule over certain canine illnesses and injuries, and how you should react.

Dog Vomiting

Dogs vomit. It's par for the course with canine care. If the idea of cleaning up the contents of a dog's stomach from time to time fills you with horror, you may need to look into an alternative line of work.

Dogs vomit for a number of reasons, and most of them are connected to food. In such cases, vomiting is the dog's way of putting things right. Reasons for a dog to vomit after eating include:

- The dog ate to excess.
- The dog ate too quickly.
- The dog moved too much – or too quickly – after eating.
- The dog food was too cold.
- The dog's stomach disagreed with an ingredient.

The temperature of dog food is more important than you may realise. Canine digestion simply cannot handle cold food, so feeding the dogs in your care straight from the fridge will not end well. Always leave food out for a couple of hours until it reaches room temperature.

If necessary, pop food in the microwave for a few seconds to remove any fridge chill. Don't heat it too long, though. A hungry dog may burn their mouth in their eagerness to tuck in, and excessive heat will kill off nutrients.

Other than this, just ensure the dogs eat slowly – and rest afterwards. Feeding the dogs in your care separately will help with this. If they do not feel like they are in competition with one another, the dogs will eat at a more sensible rate. If necessary, invest in slow feeding bowls. These can be picked up from any pet shop. They'll contain ridges that ensure a dog cannot wolf their food down in disagreeably large chunks.

Moderate a dog's food intake, too. It's a myth that dogs do not understand when they are full, or never feel that way. However, a dog's appetite is much tougher to sate than that of a human. This goes back to instinct. Wild dogs will take down sizable prey and gorge upon it, unsure as to when they'll get to eat again. Domesticated dogs know they don't need to worry about this, but instinct is a tough thing to shake off.

If a dog is vomiting outside of feeding time, ensure they have not consumed toxins. The body of a dog is similar to that of a human in this instance. It will recognise a foreign invader and look to purge it as quickly as possible. In the event of a suspected poisoning, call a vet for advice ASAP. Time may be of the essence. Never induce vomiting in the dog without being instructed to do so by a vet. If you're advised to do this, *never* place anything down a dog's throat to make them vomit. You'll need to mix hydrogen peroxide with water, to quantities advised by a professional.

Doggy Diarrhoea

If one of the dogs in your care is struggling with their stomach, it will be messy. It could also be a concerning medical condition, or just one of those things. There isn't really any way to be sure.

If a dog that you care for has diarrhoea, don't go rushing to the vet. They may run some tests, but it's such a generic symptom that it's near-impossible to know what to look for. It would be like presenting to your GP when you get a headache.

To manage a dog with diarrhoea, ensure they are cleaned up. The last thing you want is for the dog to ingest their own faeces, or for another member of the pack to do so. This will pass on any bacteria, and ensure the problem continues to spread. Watch out for dehydration when a dog has diarrhoea, too. This can be a serious problem, as we're about to discuss.

Inform the owner of the problem. They'll need to keep an eye on the dog for the rest of the day, and make a judgment call about whether to return the next day. If the diarrhoea hasn't cleared up within 24 hours, it suggests that something more sinister is afoot.

Canine Dehydration

Dehydration must never be ignored in dogs. Left untreated, dehydration can be fatal as it causes severe organ damage.

It's critical to learn the warning signs of dehydration. It usually starts with lethargy and a lack of appetite, but these are common complaints in dogs. If you suspect dehydration, pinch the skin around a dog's neck. In a healthy dog, this skin will be elasticated and spring back into position in a matter of seconds. If your dog is dehydrated, it will very slowly and steadily return to normal.

If a dog in your care is dehydrated, they must drink. Drop some broth in their water to encourage this if necessary. Electrolytes can also be helpful. You could also offer a dog a caffeine-free sports drink in an emergency, though be mindful of the sugar content of such drinks. If you reach this level of concern, it's best to see a vet. The dog may need intravenous fluids.

Aside from chronic diarrhoea, a common cause of dehydration is sunstroke. As dogs do not generate Vitamin D organically, they absorb it from the sun's rays. This means that many dogs will linger in the sun longer than is safe. You'll need to keep an eye on this and moderate the time that your canine clients spend outside during the summer. Walks will also need to be managed in times of high sun.

Canine Colds and Kennel Cough

Dogs can experience coughs, colds and sniffles, just like humans. If this is a minor cold, there is little that can be done. You cannot provide a dog with human medication, such as paracetamol. The only thing that will help is plenty of rest and water. Provide both of these by stationing the poorly dog in a private room, where they will not be disturbed. Give the dog a comfortable bed and some blankets and leave them to sleep it off.

The dog will bounce back. This could take days or weeks, depending on how infected the dog is. Just remember that viral infections spread quickly among dogs, so if you're not careful, every canine in your care will be feeling under the weather. With this mind, it's advisable to have a strict, "no sick pets" policy as part of your contract with clients. If you're not careful you'll be running an animal hospital, not a home boarding business.

One condition to be particularly careful of is Kennel Cough. As the name suggests, this is a viral condition that frequently spreads when dogs stay in kennels due to close proximity. Kennel cough is basically doggy 'flu, with the most obvious symptom being the aforementioned cough. This can be worrying to hear, as it's very loud – almost akin to a honking goose. It sounds as though the dog is gasping for breath.

Kennel cough is rarely life-threatening, but it's contagious and it will leave a dog feeling unwell for a while. What's more, owners are unlikely to happy about their dog coming home with a cough. Any vet will offer a vaccination for kennel cough, but it’s not a compulsory treatment for dog owners.

It's up to you as to whether you decide if you're willing to board dogs that have not been vaccinated against this condition. It’s worth noting that the vast majority of reputable kennels and boarding establishments now refuse to accept a dog without this vaccination, for the safety of their canine guests.

I recommend following in their footsteps, for the sake of the dogs under your care. Many local authorities require you to close for 2 weeks and carry out a deep clean in the event of an outbreak. That will significantly impact your reputation and bottom line.

Allergic Reactions

Dogs can be allergic to any number of things. It's even possible for a dog to be allergic to another animals. This is because allergies are sparked by dander – the dead skin that floats away from a shedding dog.

Survey and quiz a dog's owner about any allergies they may be living with. The good news is that allergic reactions usually come and go fairly quickly. The worst that a dog will experience is often itchy skin and hives. However, the dog will be in discomfort throughout this time. If avoidable, it's best to keep a canine from experiencing such misfortune. Not only is it sad to see, but the dog may become uncharacteristically aggressive while in discomfort.

Allergies are more serious when they impact the throat and potentially impact breathing. A common example of this is an allergy to bee or wasp stings. Dogs often encounter stinging insects while outside. Either the dog cannot resist chasing the noisy, buzzing insect, or they'll stick their nose into a nest while investigating. If a dog is allergic to a bee or wasp sting, they'll enter anaphylactic shock.

This situation requires the attention of a vet. Call for advice and see what you can do to help the dog while you're waiting to have them seen. Dogs can take Benadryl, but the safe dosage will depend upon a dog's weight and general health. It's always best to seek professional advice on this.

Conversely, even if a dog is not allergic to stings, they'll still hurt. Being stung on the paw, for example, will leave a dog feeling wholly sorry for themselves. You can help them out, but you'll need to assess whether it was a bee or wasp that did the damage. Bee stings are acidic in nature, but wasp stings are alkaline. This means that they'll be treated in different ways.

If a dog is attacked by a bee, the sting will remain in place. Never attempt to pull out the sting using your fingers or tweezers. You'll squeeze the sting, and in the process pump more venom into the dog's body. Instead, scrape the sting away using a credit card. Mix up some bicarbonate of soda with water to ease the discomfort. A wasp sting will hurt more, as wasps sting harder and deeper. Neutralise the dog's pain by mixing up vinegar and water and dabbing this on the impacted area. Once you've done so, reduce the swelling with ice.

Managing Bleeding in Dogs

When a dog starts to bleed, it can sometimes feel like they'll never stop. This is especially true if a dog is bleeding from the ear. This body part is one of the most sensitive of all canine anatomy.

To manage canine bleeding, take the following steps:

- Mix up a solution of 50% water and 50% hydrogen peroxide.

- Douse a cotton pad in this solution and tenderly dab at the bleeding area.
- Keep cleaning the wound until it's dry.
- Use a styptic pencil or powder to close up the wound. This will sting, and the dog will react. Be prepared for this.
- Bandage the wound. Secure this bandage with medical tape, not a safety pin.

The dog may need stitches if the wound is deep enough. This should be arranged by a healthcare professional.

Giving a Dog CPR

If you're extremely unlucky, you may find that a dog in your care stops breathing. This could be caused by any number of mishaps. In these cases, you may not have time to wait for a vet. Thinking – and acting – quickly could save a dog's life.

Before attempting canine CPR, you need to be certain that the dog is not breathing. Ways to confirm this include:

- Hold a finger directly in front of the dog's nose and check for breath.
- Monitor their chest for a telltale rise and fall.
- Open the dog's mouth and ensure they are no foreign objects blocking the throat.
- Check for a pulse. You can do this one of three ways.
    - Check the femoral artery. This is found at the top of the inner thigh of a dog's hind leg. Use your fingers, not your thumb, to check for a pulse here.
    - Place your thumb on the metacarpal pad (the biggest, central pad) on a dog's paw. This should throb with a heartbeat.
    - Locate the dog's heart. Lay a dog on their right-hand side and flex their front-left leg. The meeting point of the elbow and chest should lead to your dog's heart.

If your dog is not breathing, you'll need to perform CPR.

- Lay the dog flat on their right-hand side. This is important. A dog's heart is on the left of their body. Laying the dog on their right-hand side will provide significantly easier access.
- Keep the dog's back and head straight.
- Ensure the dog's tongue is forward and will not become trapped in the throat.
- Keep the dog's mouth firmly closed.
- Locate the dog's heart and perform fifteen compressions. If the dog weighs more than thirty pounds, push with your

palm. If the dog is smaller, use your fingers. Do not push too hard – you risk breaking the dog's ribs.

- After fifteen compressions, breathe once into the dog's nostrils – ensuring that dog's mouth is firmly closed.
- Repeat the above process.

If CPR has not worked within twenty minutes, it's not going to work. In addition, don't treat this as an alternative for professional treatment. Get the dog to a vet ASAP. A professional will always stand a greater chance of success.

Chapter 7

Maintaining and Growing Your Business

So, you have managed to get your business of the ground. Congratulations! That was no mean feat, and you deserve a hearty pat on the back. Offer a few pats to the dogs in your care, too. They're good boys and girls and you couldn't have done it without them.

Here's the thing, though. The hard work is only just beginning. Now that you have established your business, you need to grow and maintain it. You're unlikely to be the only person in your town with designs on working for themselves. You're also unlikely to be the only dog lover in a five-mile radius.

There will always be a new company or individual looking to undercut you and take your clients, so you need to whatever you can be ensure loyalty – and gain new business. That can be a tricky balancing act.

Never rest on your laurels. Don't sit back and think, "hey, I think I have enough clients now. If all of them stay with me, all of them pay their bills on time, and nothing untoward happens, I'm set." That's a lovely thought, but the skies are not always blue. Any of these clients could disappear at a moment's notice.

- A client's personal circumstances could change and they no longer need, or can no longer afford, your services.
- Clients can move away to a different town, or even a different country.
- Another provider may undercut you on price or start trading closer to the home of your clients.
- A dog could develop a sudden and seemingly irrational phobia of your home. This happens for a variety of reasons.
- Clients can become complacent. What does it matter if they 'forget' to pay their invoice this week? You know they're good for it, they'll square up sooner or later. This can grow problematic.
- The dog could become unwell or injured, and not be a suitable client any longer.

These are just some of the more pleasant examples. It's also possible that clients will just up and disappear on you. It's not fun when this happens, but you need to be prepared for the eventuality.

When it comes to finances and business, you're dealing with humans. Sadly, humans are not as unstintingly loyal as dogs.

So, you'll need to constantly be attracting new clients. However, you also need to be realistic about your workload and legal parameters. Don't start neglecting your existing and long-term clients in favour of the shiny new toys that come your way. Loyalty in business is a two-way street. If you want your clients to stand by you, you need to ensure that you're providing a consistently excellent service and treating a client of three years' standing as well as one of three days.

You also can't blindly promise to take on new clients when your dance card is already full. As I have previously discussed, there are legal restrictions to how many dogs you can board at any given time. If you start breaking the law here, you will face serious consequences.

Our advice is to always be looking for new clients but be honest about your availability. Set up a waiting list and make it clear that you'll be in touch the moment you can find a slot to help. As we just mentioned above, income that you rely upon could vanish at a moment's notice. Combat this by always having somebody ready to step into a vacancy.

Maintaining Your Client Base

The key to maintaining a good working relationship with your clients, both human and canine, is to keep them happy. That sounds obvious, but it's easier said than done. I'll discuss the practicalities of maintaining a harmonious client-provider relationship in a moment. In the meantime, however, let's talk about the emotional hook.

Dealing with dogs is a little different from providing other services as you're dealing primarily with emotional connection. Stop and think about your relationship with your own dog for a moment. If you were dropping them off at a daycare centre, and were faced with one of two reactions, which would you choose?

- The dog drops their ears and tail, turns sideways, and scrambles to get back into the car. You attach their leash and walk them toward the house they'll be staying at, the canine whining and generally looking miserable all the way.
- The dog starts barking excitedly and scratching at the car door from the moment you pull into a particular street. They know where they're going and could not be happier about it. Once they see their dog sitter for the day, they bound up to

them without a moment's hesitation, ignoring all previous training not to jump.

It's a no-brainer – you're going to choose the latter. Dropping off a dog with a day care provider is not like taking a reluctant child to school. The dog does not legally *need* to stay with a sitter. Unless you're making the pooch's life a pleasure, there is no reason why the owner would leave them with you. As discussed, yours will not be the only game in town.

With this in mind, the first step to maintaining clients is ensuring that the dog loves you. That shouldn't be difficult to achieve if you know how dogs operate. And if you don't, I'm a little confused as to why you're still reading this book. If canine behaviour is such an impenetrable mystery to you, why on earth did you read all that crushingly dull material about tax and pensions?

Once you have gained the trust and affection of the dog, you're well on your way to winning over their parents. Ultimately, every pet owner's priority is that their fur baby is treated well and fairly. There are other steps that you can take to keeping your human clients happy, though. Observe these six commandments of any good dog business. These are the steps that I expect anybody working under our banner to treat as critical.

- Build a Personal Relationship.
- Communicate.
- Provide Added Value.
- Show Your Expertise.
- Honour Your Commitments.
- Be Transparent.

Let's take a deeper dive into each of these.

Build a Personal Relationship

As previously discussed, there is a substantial emotional element to the relationship between you and your clients. Obviously, this needs to be managed within the confines of professionalism. You are providing a service, not necessarily looking to make friends with your human client (the dog is another matter.)

All the same, you'll forge a much stronger working relationship if you apply some personal touches. Just show that you're interested. Find out when the dog's birthday or adoption anniversary falls and send a card and order a canine-friendly cake to celebrate. Send Christmas cards to your human clients. Clear a few minutes to chat at collection and drop-off. Remember the dates that you started working together and mark the occasion by dropping it into conversation or sending a thank you email.

In many respects, just learning the name of your human client will go a long way. Dog owners become accustomed to being referred to as, "Rover's Mum" or, "Fido's Dad." Addressing somebody by name could make their day!

Above all, ensure you are always available to discuss the dog – their behaviour, their likes and dislikes, and anything you may have noticed about them. Dog owners are like parents. They feel a sense of smug satisfaction when they're informed of how well-behaved their dog was in your care. It means they are doing a good job of training. What's more, they'll be delighted to hear that dog had a good time playing with their friends. Neurotic pet owners, in particular, will feel less guilty about leaving their dog all day while working.

Communicate

Communication is essential to any relationship, and business is no exception. Keep the lines of contact open at all times, ensuring that your clients know that you can always be reached. Nobody likes to feel as though their voice goes unheard.

Some key rules of communication include:

- Never delay in responding to messages. If you can't reply in detail or answer a question just yet, settle for an acknowledgment of receipt and assurance that you'll be in touch with more detail soon.
- Don't let a phone ring out, remaining unanswered. If you know that you'll be unavailable, divert your calls to an active, personalised voicemail service. If you remain constantly unavailable, your clients may turn to somebody they feel more confident they can reach an emergency.
- If you're running late, or can't make an appointment due to sickness or a family emergency, explain this. People are understanding and will make alternative arrangements in the short-term. You're more likely to run into trouble if you just 'go dark.'

You should also use communication to improve and enhance your offering. Stay in regular touch with your clients, asking for feedback on what they feel is going well and what they think could be improved. Nobody expects you to be a mind reader. By giving clients the opportunity to share their views, you'll strengthen your working bond – as long as you act upon any reasonable suggestions!

Provide Added Value

Ultimately. keeping customers comes down to showing that you are better than your competition. A key-way to do this is offer added value to your offering, How you do this is down to you, and indeed your competitors. Learn what others are providing, and don't just match it – build upon it.

- If your competitors offer a 30-minute walk as part of their dog-sitting service, take your canine clients out for an hour.
- If your competitors work to a strict timetable, be flexible in your offering.
- If your competitors will not collect or pick up dogs, make this a key part of your service.

Price will always be a consideration when people are choosing a service provider, however. Some clients will always take the cheapest possible opinion with little to no consideration for other factors. You can't control that, so don't drop your prices to match a cheaper competitor in an attempt to maintain that client.

Success in business is not a race to the bottom, and you should focus your attention on customers that value their dogs. We're working with living, sentient beings here, and you should only look to do business with people that acknowledge and understand this.

Show Your Expertise

You may recall that I listed some recommended training courses earlier in this book. That's for your own benefit. Knowledge and expertise can be a great way to keep clients on-side.

Your customers will always feel more secure if they are leaving their pooch with somebody that knows the ins and outs of their chosen business. It's up to you to prove that you're at the top of the tree when it comes to identifying and managing canine behaviour and wellness.

Ultimately, if your clients trust you and consider you to be an expert, they'll stick with you. Everybody wants to leave their pet with a safe pair of hands. If you merge this professional expertise with the personal touch that I previously described, you'll enjoy a long and fruitful business relationship.

Honour Your Commitments

It's easy to make promises in the heat of the moment. This may mean that yourself agreeing to 'favours' for your clients as you feel like you're on the spot.

That's not ideal, but you really need to follow through on those promises. Don't retract the offer – or worse yet, outright change your mind and refuse to help –when you realise that it will be inconvenient for you. That can irreparably damage a working relationship.

It's a sad fact of life that some clients will always extract the urine. You'll be expected to go the extra mile on occasion, and that's fair enough. As I've previously explained, added value is always a winner. Sometimes, however, your additional efforts will become the expectation rather than a grateful bonus.

In these instances, you'll need to think long and hard about the cost of doing business. If somebody is expecting an extra couple of hours of work from you and not paying for the privilege, question whether you're happy for that to become a regular arrangement. Here's a hint – you shouldn't be.

Ultimately, you should treat all of your clients fairly. If Client A pays you for 8 hours of work that's what you provide, it's not really on to provide Client B with 10 hours of service for the same price. Eventually, you may need to part ways. Attempt to communicate and negotiate a compromise first, though.

Be Transparent

Nobody likes to feel like somebody is trying to pull the wool over their eyes. Be honest and transparent with your clients at all times. That involves financial and care issues.

Let's start with invoicing. Always be clear and upfront about what you're charging – and why. If you plan to increase your prices, you're more than entitled to do so. It's your business. Just communicate this in advance and make it clear why you're doing so. It's then down to the client to decide if they'll retain your services.

Be honest in the event of a mishap with a client's dog, too. Never try to cover up an injury and hope it goes unnoticed. This will not happen. Dog owners know that their pets get themselves into all manner of pickles and will likely be understanding if you explain that something unfortunate befell them. Explain what happened – and how – and what you did to resolve the problem. That will always go further than pleading ignorance.

This transparency also covers canine behaviour. If the dog refused to go for a walk with you, tell the owner. There may be a reason that requires investigation, such as a leg problem. It's equally possible that the dog was just in a lazy mood. Either way, just *tell your client*. If their dog constantly comes home filled with unfulfilled energy, they'll start to wonder just what goes on while you're taking care of them.

This transparency may cost you business on occasion. That's unfortunate. It's considerably better than losing clients through *dis*honesty, though. Word of mouth is arguably the most powerful marketing tool of all. If you develop a reputation among the dog-loving community as somebody not to be trusted, your reputation will be in serious trouble.

Attracting New Clients

As we have discussed, keeping your existing clients happy is paramount. You'll still need to think one step ahead, though.

There's a universal truth that all business owners and operators will share. When you're fully booked and doing well, people will be falling over themselves to hire you. When the chips are down and you're looking for clients to keep yourself afloat, it can become extremely tricky to drum up new business.

The indisputable truth is that, unless people know about you and your offering, you won't attract new business. As I just said, word of mouth can be hugely beneficial. If you offer a good service, people talk. Dog owners, in particular, exchange information. A good reputation can be worth its weight in gold among pet care circles. Everybody is always looking for a reliable dogsitter or walker.

You can't rely on your clients to do all the work for you, though. You'll need to roll up your sleeves and start attracting clients for yourself. That means launching a two-pronged attack of traditional, offline marketing and selling your services over the Internet.

Don't neglect one of these approaches in favour of the other. Regardless of what anybody tells you, not everything is conducted online. Equally, however, placing your entire trust in the offline world is a risky proposition in the 21st Century.

Marketing Your Business Offline

Raising awareness for your business offline takes three primary forms.

- Print advertisements and posters.
- Leaflets and flyers.
- Business cards.

Let's start by discussing business cards. Yes, these are still in circulation. In fact, business cards remain possibly the easiest way to insert yourself into the consciousness of potential clients.

The glory of a business card is that it can contain all the information you need in a small, compact space. You can tell people your web address until you're blue in the face, but having it written down means they're much more likely to actually remember. Handing out these cards means that you're playing the long game, ensuring that you're in somebody's mind before they even realise they'll need you.

Naturally, the compact nature of business cards means that you can also carry them anywhere you may need. A business card can be kept in a wallet or purse until needed. This means you can always have a stack on your person.

- Sitting in the waiting room of the vet? Strike up a conversation with your fellow dog owners and let them know what you do.
- Out for a stroll with your canine clients? Respond to the inevitable, "you've got your hands full there!" comments by handing over a business card and explaining that you're always happy to take on more responsibility.
- Attending an animal care-related event or exhibition? Frankly, people will think less of you if you don't have a business card to share.

There are still certain rules of engagement that apply with business cards. If you're not careful, you can come across as a little *American Psycho* if you try to foist it upon unsuspecting recipients. If you feel that somebody is interested in what you have to offer, however, a business card can be pivotal. They may not take you up on your services immediately, but they'll have your contact information for when they need you.

The same also applies to leaflets and flyers. On the surface, these marketing techniques are completely outdated. Let's be blunt – they're frequently a nuisance. Fortunately for you, they can also be surprisingly impactful in the long-term.

Arrange for a flyer run that advertises your services. Keep the design simple, and skip out on any frills, but have at least one eye-catching and memorable feature. Brightly coloured paper is a good choice. Explain what you do, how much your charge to do it, and how people can get hold of you.

Get these leaflets pushed through the doors of your local area, either delivering them yourself or arranging for somebody to do it for you. Arrange a limited print run, and don't spend too much money. You're unlikely to get any business out of the first drop.

"But wait!" I hear you cry. "If this will not attract any business, and it will just annoy people, why bother at all?"

The truth is, flyers – like business cards – are an exercise in playing the long game. It's a short-term loss for potential long-term gain. After three months or so, arrange for the same leaflet to be delivered to the same properties. Yes, there is every chance that the occupants will just throw it away. You may end up shoved in a drawer, though. This is better news than you may think.

You see, the more you repeat this action, the more you are imprinting yourself on the memory of the recipients. Eventually, they may well need the services of a doggy day care facility, boarder or dog walker. When they do, the conversation will invariably turn to your flyer. "Do we still have that leaflet? You know, the yellow one that kept coming through the door? I'm sure that was for a dog walker. Check the junk drawer, give them a ring if you find it."

Obviously you won't be able to sustain a long-term business or attract all the new clients that you'll need by flyering and leafleting alone. You'll also need to weigh up the cost implications of print runs and the time and labour of delivering them against any potential work that you may attract. You're not obligated to arrange a leaflet or flyer run if it's not economically astute. Just be aware that you may be surprised at how effective this approach can be.

Finally, we have good old-fashioned print advertising. This could take two forms:

- Advertisements in the local newspaper or parish magazine.
- Posters in the window of your newsagent, post office and other such locations.

Never underestimate how impactful a poster can be, especially if strategically placed. Newsagent windows will always attract a certain type of client, but forge relationships elsewhere too so you can place your posters in a variety of places. Ask the vet if you can put up posters in their waiting room. Speak to your local town council and ask the clerk to place them in the notice boards frequented by dog walkers. Arrange for the posters to placed at the school gates, where exhausted-looking parents congregate. Pin them up in doctor's waiting rooms, and at your local barber shop, where people will be sat waiting and taking in their surroundings. People will relish the opportunity to take at least one responsibility off their to-do list by hiring you.

There is very much a market for offline advertising and marketing. With it being the 21st Century, however, you do still owe it to yourself to get online and sell your wares via the internet.

Marketing Your Business Online

When many people think about advertising their business online, they think about having a website. That's a good idea – in theory.

The truth is though, websites can take a lot of work to maintain. Having a bad website in the modern age is worse than having no website at all. If you're not particularly comfortable with the vagaries of the online world, skip the website if you really must, but 85% of folks search online.

You can get away with turning Facebook into your Internet home. A well-stacked and informative Facebook page will attract plenty of interest and might shoot to the top of any Google search rankings. You can also spread the word about your business quite easily. Invite friends to like and share your page, and if necessary, pay for additional advertising.

To pay or not to pay is an eternal dilemma for small businesses on Facebook. The reality is, the site administrators do not make it easy for businesses to reach their target audiences without paid advertisements. You may find that posts from your business page fail to appear in many news feeds. The way to avoid this is to boost interaction. The more people that like and share your posts, the more likely they are to see them more often in the future. Naturally, in order to encourage people to do just that, you'll need to create content worthy of liking and sharing.

Don't neglect your Facebook page. Nurture and update it multiple times a day. Everybody loves photos of dogs doing doggy things. Post regular snapshots of your canine clients and their escapades, making it obvious that they're having the time of their life, but ensure you have your client's prior written consent. There is no form of advertising that's more potent and appealing than animals having fun.

If you decide that a website is the way to go, that's fine too. Just be aware that you need to manage and maintain it. There are plenty of software programmes that will build the structure for you, and you can fill it however you want.

If you decide to advertise your business through your website, refer back to our previous conversation about differentiating yourself from your competition and adding value. Consider what you can add to a website to ensure that people consider you a trustworthy guardian for their furry bundle of joy. Some suggestions of what you could add include:

- Blogs and diary entries of your work with existing clients.
- Personal blog entries that shine a light on the person behind the business.
- Records of any charity or social work that you perform with your dogs.
- Interesting and informative articles on canine healthcare.

Basically, a website is more than just a sale's tool. It should be a window into your offering, your personality and your life. That's the stuff that will convince people to put their hands in their pockets and pay for your services.

There's one other thing to note when setting up a website. The temptation will always be to pick up a new domain name from a provider like GoDaddy. After all, that's the most cost-effective and unique way of doing things. Don't underestimate the impact of purchasing an existing but defunct domain name.

If you're looking to drum up new business through the internet, you'll be using Google to do so. Like it or not, that's the platform that the vast majority of people use to search for services. People also rarely scroll past the first few matches on the page. This means you need to be as high up those rankings as possible.

Now, attempting to understand Google's ever-changing algorithms is an exercise in futility. The goalposts move every few months and attempting to build a website that stays in Google's good graces is akin to spinning a roulette wheel. One thing that always helps is having an older domain name, though. If a domain has been in existence for three years – especially if it attracts traffic – it will be boosted by Google when people search.

Admittedly, that's not *such* a concern for a website in this particular niche. Somebody searching for, "home boarding + TOWN NAME" will not necessarily be met with an avalanche of matches. If there are two of three competing sites, however, it pays to be the one on the top. Dazzle a visitor sufficiently with your site, and they won't even bother viewing any others. Sometimes, paying a little extra for the right domain name can lead to considerably greater profits further down the line.

Chapter 8

Concluding Thoughts and Summary

Well, you made it. Sincere thanks for taking the time to read everything that I have had to say throughout the pages of this book. That suggests the kind of hardiness and commitment necessary to start and grow a successful dog business.

Before I wrap up, however, it's probably pertinent to summarise everything that has been discussed thus far. I have hit you with a lot of information and wouldn't blame you if you were feeling slightly dazed and confused.

Read on for some closing thoughts, a weblink for some more useful information and a breakdown of how you can make your dog boarding business a success.

Stage Zero – Is This for You?

Yes, I'm asking this again. I'm pretty sure that you know the answer by now. You'd have to be some kind of masochist to have read this entire book if you're still on the fence about whether a dog boarding business is the one for you. All the same, an important question always bears repeating.

Do not open your doors to dogs – or put yourself through the lengthy and frequently frustrating legal processes of starting your business – unless you are absolutely certain that you're in this for the long haul. It will be hard and exhausting work, it will sometimes feel like a thankless task, and on more than one occasion you'll likely sit with your head in your hands and wonder why you ever thought this was a good idea. If that doesn't sound appealing, think twice.

Just remember though – those moments will be outnumbered by amazing alternatives, and you'll be making fantastic memories each and every day. All the same, you're asking a lot of yourself, and your family, by taking up this line of work. Dogs are not always considerate lodgers. You'll need to ensure that everybody living in your home is completely onboard.

So, are you physically fit enough to keep up with a pack of demanding dogs?

Are you financially ready to run the gauntlet of concerns and complications that come with running your own business?

Are you emotionally able to deal with the fact that you'll fall in love with these canine companions, and yet they'll come and go from your life?

Is your sense of humour sturdy enough to survive the whirlwind of chaos that you're inviting into your life?

If you answered yes to all these questions, congratulations. You're ready for Stage One, and you're one step closer to launching your home dog business.

Stage One – DIY or DIWY?

DIY (Do It Yourself)
Decide whether you're happy to go it alone and immerse yourself in the many points covered in this book - and why not? Many have.

DIWY (Do It With You)
I know some dog lovers and aspiring dog business owners that find all that needs to be successfully negotiated just too daunting. Don't let that put you off. Remember, where there's a will, there's a way.

Do It With You means you can still make your dream a reality by becoming a franchise partner where the franchisor holds your hand through every step of the journey and helps ensure you minimise the chances of failure.

One of my businesses, MyWaggyTails offers just such a franchise partnership. For more information see the helpful links at the end of this book.

Stage Two – Bone up on the Legal Stuff

The next step of your journey is ensuring that you're legally compliant in every step of the dog boarding business. Remember, failing to abide by the law of the land will not just earn you a slap on the wrist. You'll be staring down the barrel of hefty fines, the retraction of your license, the loss of your business, and possibly even a custodial sentence.

Check that you can run a business from your home without landing yourself in trouble. Ensure that your neighbours will not kick up a fuss and cause issues for you and your business. Double- and triple-check that all your home insurers and service providers are aware that you're running a business.

Next, look into the many and varied insurance policies that you're going to need. Crunch the numbers and make sure that these monthly expenses are sustainable. Yes, you can claim them back on your tax return – but that's a whole year away. You'll need to be making your monthly commitments to keep these policies active. If you allow them to lapse, you may be putting yourself in legal hot water.

If you're confident that you have ticked everything associated with these boxes, it's time to start thinking about permits and licenses. Read up on what kind of business you're looking to run. Terminology matters, and one wrong word could completely change the complexion of your business.

Once you're ready, make an initial appointment with the powers-that-be at your local council. Ensure that you do not leave their office until every conceivable question that you can think of has been answered to your satisfaction. After that, you're ready for Stage Three.

Stage Three – Prepare Your Home

Once your home becomes your place of business, you need to make certain adjustments. You're going to be inspected before licenses and permits can be finalised, so you'll save yourself a lot of work and aggravation by taking the appropriate steps in advance.

Remind yourself of the criteria for legally compliant canine care and do whatever is necessary to meet these needs. Don't wait to be told to make changes – be proactive. Once you've done that, take things to another level. Wander around your house and ask yourself the same question time and time again. "Is that safe for dogs?"

Once you're confident that you can bring dogs into your home, you can move along. You're still not ready to contact clients, though. As Stage Four explains, you're still knee-deep in the educational element of your dog day care journey.

Stage Four – Study and Learn

Now that you have come this far, it's time to complete your education. Get yourself booked onto classes, watch as many online videos as you can, ask to spend time with experienced dog boarders, and basically learn everything there is to know about the business that you're getting into.

You don't just want to be legally compliant. That's a necessity, but it's also just a starting point. Why would you want to settle for achieving the bare minimum? You will surely want to create the best possible offering for your clients.

Once you feel that you have learned everything there is to know about dogs, canine boarding and business, you're really cooking with gas. You can move onto Stage Five, and there's no turning back from there.

Stage Five – Register Your Business

Take a deep breath – things are about to get official. Refer back to our chapter on the differences between operating as a sole trader and a limited company and decide what will meet your needs best. I recommend starting out as a sole trader, but as always, the decision is entirely yours.

Once you've registered your business, you need to get serious. Think about how you are going to tackle the needs of your clients and start drawing up timetables and budget plans. Think about whether you are going to need to hire additional help – the chances are that you will – and look into where you'll find that.

Also remember – from the moment you register as a company, you're no longer off the grid or flying under radar. HMRC know who you are, and they know what you do for a living. This means that Stage Six becomes critical.

Stage Six – Lay Your Tax and Employee Groundwork

Nobody likes to think about taxes, but you're going to need to get straight in this regard. Get your Tax Identifier Number and start saving a percentage of your earnings. January 31st is set to become the most expensive date in your calendar. It's advisable to open a separate bank account for your taxes and to stockpile the money here. If you can get an account with a high interest rate, so much the better. You may as well benefit from being a law-abiding citizen.

It's not just tax that you need to consider, though. If you are getting help from other people, you may need to pay them a pension. They'll also have a variety of rights that you'll be expected to meet. Knowing the difference between an employee and a worker, and communicating this with your assistants, could make a huge difference to your bottom line.

It can take a while to get your head around tax, pensions and everything involved. Take your time, and make sure that you're completely aware of everything that's expected of you. This is not an act first and beg forgiveness situation later. If you need a break from all that dry stuff, you could always make a start on Stage Seven. Before you can bring any canine clients into your home, you'll need to have strict policies in place to protect yourself and your business.

Stage Seven – Devise Your Policies

If you're going to be doing business, you need to think like a businessperson. That means having clear, unbreakable policies in place. If you can draw up a contract for your clients, so much the better.

There's a lot to think about here, so take your time and give your policies plenty of consideration. You need to weigh up the safety and treatment of the dogs, while also ensuring that your own needs are being met. You'll need to keep your clients happy, but don't allow the balance of power to slip too far away from you. The occasional favour is fine, but you *are* running a business.

This is the key thing in mind while drawing up your policies. You embarked on this journey because you wanted the freedom of self-employment, and to break free of the constraints of the nine-to-five.

You'll need to be flexible – a big part of leaving that aforementioned nine-to-five is that you don't work such rigid hours, for good or ill. Just make sure that you're going to benefit from this career path. After all, if you're still living your life according to the whims of others, what's the point?

Stage Eight – Open Your Doors!

On paper, it's that simple. You're now in business. I won't say sit back and relax – that's quite the opposite of how your days will look. Do stop to take a moment and pat yourself on the back though. Look at the dogs in your home and prepare yourself for your new life.

Stage Nine – Grow Your Business

Once you have clients on your books, you're off to a great start. That's all this is, though – the start. Nobody ever built a successful empire by resting on their laurels and assuming that their work was done.

Look into ways that you boost your business, attracting a steady stream of new clients while simultaneously keeping your loyal customers happy. Always have a waiting list of potential clients in case something happens to one of your regulars. Do not rely on everybody on your books remaining that way forever. Things happen, and you'll need to be ready to roll with the punches. Life has a habit of throwing curveballs, after all.

Once you have built your business and you're enjoying a roaring trade, it's time to take a well-deserved holiday and celebrate your success.

This brings us to the end of *Home from Home*. One final time – thank you for even considering taking this journey with us. Whatever your future holds, I wish you – and the special tail-wagging chums in your life – the very best of health, prosperity and good fortune. And just remember – a dog is for life, and if done properly, so is a dog business.

Helpful Links

As I mentioned earlier, this weblink provides a number of useful resources and information for the aspiring dog business owner.

Visit DogBusiness.co.uk/links

Here you will find useful resources on:

- Licensing Guidelines
- Professional Dog Walking Guidelines
- Guide to Canine Welfare
- Franchising
- Courses and resources
- Forms, policies, check lists, service agreements
- Insurance
- Dog business website builder

About the Author

Randle Stonier - After a career which included life as a Royal Navy officer, a stint in the Metropolitan Police and working for both Procter & Gamble and Sir Richard Branson's Virgin Group, Randle spent most of his career working in, starting up and growing several marketing and events agencies, invariably with a dog or two at his side.

A few years ago, together with his sister Mitch he set up MyWaggyTails, initially as a home boarding, home day care and dog walking business. He later decided to help others to achieve their dreams by providing franchise partnerships in MyWaggyTails.

Randle is also the host of the 'From Wags to Riches' podcast and most recently launched the Dog Business School – providing a range of courses and resources for dog professionals. He is closely supervised by Ebs, the flat-coated retriever.

Printed in Dunstable, United Kingdom

67784671R00061